Praise for *Perfectly You*

"Mariana inspires the next generation of women to carve their own paths and dare to be themselves. *Perfectly You* is a must-read for women everywhere!"

—Eva Longoria Bastón
Actress, philanthropist, and businesswoman

"*Perfectly You* is a tribute to our American story. Like so many of our journeys, Mariana's quest is an example that when you hold your culture up high and embrace the road ahead . . . you can contribute to the American dream."

—Wilmer Valderrama
Actor, producer, and activist

"Mariana Atencio is among the clearest, strongest, and most important voices of her generation. She powerfully relates truths about what it means to be an immigrant and a citizen, how to cope with loss and embrace an uncertain but limitless future. This book is essential reading for everyone who dares to dream."

—Joy-Ann Reid
Host of *AM Joy* on MSNBC

"Mariana Atencio is the next-gen voice breaking all barriers."

—Jorge Ramos
Anchor for the Univision network and author

"What I love about Mariana is the joy she exudes in her life and in her profession. What you'll appreciate in her memoir is learning just how important it is to believe in yourself deeply. It may be the only thing we have. We are lucky Mariana has chosen to share her story so that we are all able to see how perfect we already are."

—Maria Hinojosa
CEO of Futuro Media Group
Anchor and executive producer of Latino USA

"[Mariana] tells her readers not to get discouraged and to keep pursuing their dreams—without forgetting who they are in the process."

—People

"As America's need for reliable journalism grows, so too has Mariana's voice as a journalist: one that embodies America's aspirations and empowers our mission to hold power accountable."

—Ali Velshi
MSNBC anchor
Business correspondent for NBC News and MSNBC

"Despite the often dark nature of some of the stories she covers, Atencio has been known to keep a sunny disposition, which is best embodied by the #GoLikeMariana hashtag she uses to connect with her audience on social media. *Perfectly You* is a continuation of that."

—Refinery29

"Mariana's story is our story. A journalist's memoir of self-discovery shaped in part by the people she encounters on her many travels to tell their stories. *Perfectly You* is inspirational and aspirational. Mariana teaches us that success is not about where you start but how you finish."

—Hugo Balta
President of the National Association of Hispanic Journalists (NAHJ)

Perfectly You

EMBRACING THE POWER OF BEING REAL

MARIANA ATENCIO

W PUBLISHING GROUP

AN IMPRINT OF THOMAS NELSON

Published in Nashville, Tennessee, by W Publishing, an imprint of Thomas Nelson.

Thomas Nelson titles may be purchased in bulk for educational, business, fund-raising, or sales promotional use. For information, please email SpecialMarkets@ThomasNelson.com.

Any Internet addresses, phone numbers, or company or product information printed in this book are offered as a resource and are not intended in any way to be or to imply an endorsement by Thomas Nelson, nor does Thomas Nelson vouch for the existence, content, or services of these sites, phone numbers, companies, or products beyond the life of this book.

ISBN 978-0-7852-2903-2 (eBook)
ISBN 978-0-7852-2838-7 (HC)

Library of Congress Cataloging-in-Publication Data

Library of Congress Control Number: 2019902661

Printed in the United States of America

19 20 21 22 23 LSC 10 9 8 7 6 5 4 3 2 1

For Papi. Love is infinite; so is our bond.

The word *perfection* needs to be redefined. It's not the absence of flaws, but the commitment to give our best in everything we do.

—MARIANA

Contents

CONTENTS

Foreword

Perfectly You: The Power of Authenticity

Have you ever had an identity crisis? I have. But it's not what you're thinking. It wasn't born out of a sense of not knowing who I am or not accepting myself. Rather, like so many other people, I've gone through that inner battle between being myself or living up to the expectations that others have of me. When we are children, we want to please our parents and our teachers and be accepted by our classmates. As teenagers, peer pressure sets in; many times we succumb to it. By the time we get to college—a period in our lives when we really begin to shape our identities and our journeys— the temptation to placate and heed our parents' desires hits us front and center. And suddenly, our lives take off. But where to? Some of us spend a lifetime searching for our own identities, trying to understand and, more importantly, accept ourselves. When we finally do, we become unstoppable.

Perfectly You is the title Mariana Atencio chose for this book. I think it's because after undergoing all of these stages herself, she realized that there is nothing more powerful than being authentic. And if you really dare to hold your own, you get to know yourself; put aside your insecurities, doubts, and fears; and not allow anyone or anything to intimidate you.

Forging this path is even more challenging for Latinos in the US, whether you are an immigrant or the son or daughter of immigrants, as I am. I was born in Los Angeles to Mexican parents. That duality brings another type of identity crisis. There's a moment in our lives where we simply don't know if we are from here or from there. We wonder if it is the color of our passport or the color of our skin that determines who we are. Or rather, if it is our flag or the blood of our ancestors to whom we owe allegiance. When we realize that, in fact, it is a combination of all of these things and emotions that defines us, we can finally begin to enjoy being special.

This is how I feel. I am extremely proud of my heritage, of having been raised bilingual and bicultural. I feel fortunate to have been able to grow up in a world where the sounds, aromas, and colors of two worlds become intertwined into one.

But it's not all a bed of roses. No matter how much pride we have in our cultural heritage, we often have to face rejection, contempt, discrimination, and intimidation, precisely because of our ethnic origin. And as if that weren't enough, that insecurity we thought we had overcome returns in full force. Some call it *impostor syndrome*. Have you heard of it? It seeps through the cracks right when we achieve something, and suddenly, we think we don't deserve it.

I have my story. If I had to summarize it in a few words, I would say that it is a story of triumph and perseverance. Why? First of all, because I grew up in a low-income family in Los Angeles, and I had to start working in a sweatshop at the age of fourteen to help my parents pay the bills. Second, because I had to break into a profession where women have to work twice as hard to receive half the recognition that men do. To achieve it, I had to triumph over adversity and be very, very persevering.

As a journalist, I have dedicated my life to telling other people's stories. There are tales of struggle, sadness, suffering, and despair, of hate and rejection. But I have also told stories of success, survival, kindness, solidarity, and empathy.

I've told so many stories that I know all too well that we all have one. After all, it's our stories that mark us, define us, and become our true north. In this book we discover the story of Mariana Atencio: the woman, immigrant, daughter, sister, wife, journalist, and friend.

Although she is still very young and has a bright future ahead, she knows who she is and is discovering what she wants to do with her life. She is determined to leave a mark. She wants not only to make a difference in her life and career but also to share what she has learned along the way and put it at the service of others, hoping it will help them in their own journeys. That's called *leadership*. It's when you understand that it's not only about your path but helping to pave the way for others.

—María Elena Salinas

Introduction

New York City, 2013

It finally happened!

I was invited to appear on one of the most famous shows in the world: *Good Morning America.*

I'd been hired by Fusion, a groundbreaking network for Millennials cocreated by Spanish-language giant Univision and Disney's iconic ABC, to cohost a new show. Fusion was a bold experiment whose mission was to create news and entertainment for our generation in an irreverent way. In a stroke of luck, I had auditioned for the big honchos at both networks and was hired.

Honestly, I don't even know how I got chosen. I had never auditioned for anything in my life! The other talent trying out included celebrities, comedians, and former White House communications staffers, since politics would be a big part of the channel's DNA. I felt like everyone there was "somebody"—a list of who's who. Meanwhile, I was the underdog, a young Latina immigrant whose first language was Spanish and who just wanted to break through.

By some miracle—which I attribute to my not having anything to lose—I got the job. Now, along with my future coanchors Pedro Andrade, a famous model and journalist from Brazil, and Yannis Pappas, a successful stand-up comedian from Brooklyn, I was going to appear on *GMA*—live from Times Square, *mi gente*—to talk about our new show. It would be my first time on English-speaking television.

This was the big leagues, but nobody could have warned this twenty-nine-year-old woman originally from Venezuela that the day was not going to be as perfect as she'd dreamed.

I'd caught the last flight out of Miami the night before and had barely slept a wink. Everything had to be flawless. After getting so far, what could go wrong?

That morning, I got up at 5:00 a.m. sharp, blasted some '90s merengue music, and brushed my teeth while showering. (It's a habit; no time to waste.) I was determined to be at the *GMA* studios by 7:00 a.m.

After careful consideration, I selected a mustard-colored top and a black skirt, what I considered my best pair of shoes, and classic jewelry. From what I gathered, women on English-language networks had a much more subdued appearance, and even though we were representing a younger audience, I wanted to look the part.

I slipped on my favorite pair of flats to spare my feet from walking the streets of the Big Apple in high heels. I wanted to walk all the way to Times Square, from the apartment my parents kept uptown. I needed the time to organize my thoughts.

On my way I stopped by St. Patrick's Cathedral to say a little prayer and give thanks for my many blessings. Every time I'm in New York, I try to go by and light a candle for the Virgin of Guadalupe, Mexico's patron saint. Thousands make the 2,500-mile pilgrimage to her altar from Mexico to New York every December, in a trek known as the procession of *La Guadalupana*. My devotion to the Virgin of Guadalupe began in childhood Christmas trips to that beautiful country, where Papi, my dad—my foundation—taught us the meaning of faith.

Growing up, I trusted his practical and spiritual teachings. He always reminded me, "No matter where you may be on your journey, be grateful for where you have been and where you are going."

I felt him there with me that morning in New York, even though he was all the way in Caracas, the capital of my home country, where I grew up. Though I'd come the two thousand miles by plane and not on foot, I would need plenty of grace on this pilgrimage of my own, all the way from South America to Manhattan.

Somewhere in those seemingly endless blocks, it became clear I'd made my first mistake on my "flawless" day. When I arrived at the *GMA* studios in Times Square, I looked down to see my swollen, blistered feet. Mustering a somewhat confident smile, I limped past the security guards, trying to figure out which elevator to take.

Once I found the right one and stepped inside, I saw my

reflection in the elevator door. A jolt of adrenaline hit me. The bracelet with my name engraved on it, which my *abuela* had gifted me as a child, was missing from my right wrist. *No, no, no, esto sí que no—this cannot be happening.*

I'm often juggling so many things that I don't focus on what's right in front of me. My maternal grandma wasn't one who usually gave us presents; this beloved heirloom was one of the few things she had ever given me. Now I was faced with a stark choice: go back to try to find *abuela*'s bracelet, or go forward toward the job of my dreams.

I thought about what my mom would do in my place. She'd probably turn back. It pained me, but I wanted this job more.

By the time the elevator doors opened, I had my made my choice.

"¿Me indica dónde está el baño, por favor?" I asked a lady passing by where I could find a restroom, and her blank stare made me realize I was speaking Spanish. I repeated the question in English.

When I reached the bathroom, it was 6:38 a.m. That gave me a bit of time to make myself presentable and cover my blisters with Band-Aids while hoping not to have another setback. Then I put on my black pumps. Wearing them was pure torture.

I was sent to the makeup room, and the artist who helped me gave me some advice about trying a new look—thinner eyebrows and shorter, possibly lighter hair—for when my show would debut the following week. "It could be a nice change. Highlights do wonders to light up your face."

I hadn't given a thought to my look beyond clothing and accessories. Would I need to find a different style? I had no clue; I only knew I didn't want to change to fit in. So I thanked her and left.

Wobbling my way to a break room, I saw some of the hosts of *GMA*: George Stephanopoulos, Lara Spencer, Josh Elliott, and Sam Champion. In a few minutes they would give us precious airtime to reach millions of households all over America. I stood there, bagel in hand and throbbing feet, starstruck and feeling the dreaded impostor's syndrome. What could I contribute here next to these beloved figures?

As I was introduced to some of the staff, the most basic task—trying to get my name pronounced correctly—became an ordeal. Some attempts quickly escalated from *Mary-Anna* or *Maria* to *Marina* and what I thought sounded like a muffled *Marinara*.

Reaching sauce status was enough to make me give up. *Maria* would work for now. I didn't want anything to rattle me before we went out there. I was ready to face Times Square.

Every morning the hosts come outside and talk to people who have traveled from all over the country, hoping to be on TV for a couple of minutes.

I remember the loud cheering, the sound of cabs honking in the distance, the producers giving directions all around, cameras everywhere. It was overwhelming. I wasn't used to working with street noise. I couldn't make out what anyone was saying.

I saw the floor manager signal for me to move to the left, then to the right. I had the crowd's voices in my ear. It all happened so fast. That's the pace of live television.

Two blinks later, George Stephanopoulos (who was such a big deal that he'd inspired a character on *The West Wing*) had put a mic in our faces. Nobody had told us who would be asked what or when. And there was the added complication that Pedro, Yannis, and I hadn't worked together yet. We had met a few weeks before, but we hadn't developed the kind of chemistry that you see on morning TV, which often takes years to master and would come later.

I stood back and watched Yannis joke around with George about being Greek. Pedro mentioned he'd be in bed by 7:00 p.m., watching *The Golden Girls* reruns.

Meanwhile, I was panicking. Nobody was talking about our show, how people could watch it, or why this joint venture was so important that both Univision and ABC were making a synchronized launch in their morning shows.

Finally, Lara turned to me, and I started explaining all I could think of. I was so stressed out; I felt the need to fill the air—literally—with what I considered to be relevant information about Fusion and our show.

Before I knew it, the segment was over. We were asked to stay with chef Guy Fieri for eating and banter. Three barbecue chickens later, we were done. *Phew!* I'd spilled a little BBQ sauce on my shirt, but at least I didn't accidently answer anything in Spanish. Mission accomplished!

Later that morning the president of Disney-ABC, Ben Sherwood, called us up to his office. I was excited. He was a visionary who had written the novel that the movie *Charlie St. Cloud* was based on, and he'd reimagined TV several times. I thought he was about to congratulate us.

Instead he looked at the three of us—especially at me—and said, "Well . . . that was a missed opportunity."

My heart sank. I wanted to die. *Ay no, Mariana. You were afraid that you'd mess up, and you did.*

Mr. Sherwood went on to explain that we hadn't taken into consideration the audience we were speaking to. He suggested we should have said something along the lines of, "If you want to know what your son or daughter is watching, what they like, what they're up to, tune in to our show."

As soon as I heard him say it, I understood he was right. It was an enormous lesson that I would never forget: always know your audience and prepare to speak to them.

I walked out devastated.

I couldn't get over the morning's failure. I didn't even feel comfortable asking Yannis or Pedro what they thought. They had much more experience than me and probably understood that it was more important to make a connection with the viewers than blurt out talking points. In my mind, I had totally botched it, and the big boss knew it.

What was I going to do now?

After the morning's flurry of activity, I finally had a moment to sit and look through my phone. Dozens of messages popped up from all over: Venezuela, Mexico, Los Angeles, and many other cities in the United States.

"*Hola*, Mariana, I'm José. I have followed you since you started your career, and I wanted to say that you are a great inspiration to many young people." Another message read, "Mariana, you don't know me, but I've followed you since Univision, and it was so inspiring to see you, one of us, on English TV. *¡Qué orgullo!*"

I spent the next hour browsing through social media. I read lots of motivational comments that slowly restored my confidence and reminded me of my purpose. The minute I walked out that door, a tiny spark of rebelliousness activated my real inner voice: *You got here because of your personality, and that's the only way you will stand out. You messed up; learn from it and keep moving forward. They hired Mariana, not Maria or someone else.*

I realized I had something valuable to share. Sure, there would definitely be a learning curve—but that's a part of every challenge. It's a part of life.

When starting a new job, a new class at school, or changing careers, so many of us think, *Am I really qualified for this? Maybe they've made a mistake choosing me.* When I'm in that position, I try to see myself the way José saw me: through the eyes of his generation, which is the most connected, diverse, and empathetic the world has ever seen. They know that each one of us has more to offer than we think. They appreciate what makes all of us special and why perfection as we describe it is overrated. Those messages put things into perspective.

That spark was the birthplace of this book. You see, my first day on an English-speaking network was not what I'd hoped for. Neither was I as perfect as I wanted to be. But, as my parents taught me so well, I can only be perfectly me. I was where I was as a result of all the things that had happened to me—good and bad, wanted and unwanted, perfect and *oh so* imperfect. These are the things that make us who we are, that give us the tools we need to face life's battles.

It's not easy to be comfortable with every decision we've made. Even now, several years after the *GMA* lesson, I wonder how I became one of the few Latina national correspondents or anchors and, to my knowledge, the first from Venezuela currently working at MSNBC. It's all been an unpredictable and fascinating journey. After all, people who cross over from Spanish-language media are few and far between. The pool of talent usually comes from local news or is poached from other English-speaking stations. Even though I was hired from Univision with five years of network experience and had won the prestigious Peabody Award, I still had an accent and was relatively unknown in the general market. And yet, so many things off and on screen contributed to where I am today and will contribute to where I want go from here.

Every time I share my story, people connect with some of my aha moments, so I started sharing them on social media, adding #GoLikeMariana as a personal touch in some of my posts. I created a hashtag that meant "keep going forward" in a fun way. I wanted to motivate myself with positive reinforcement. Those "go like" actions have helped me take on life as it comes and make the best of it.

So my first big break in English actually *was* perfect—blisters and blunders included—because it's what I needed to remember who I was. It's not about comparing yourself to others but comparing yourself to who you were, where you started, and where you're going.

When you're standing on the other side of that big door, the gateway to your dreams, no one else really knows what it's taken to get there.

In this book, I hope to share with you some of my hardships, lessons, fears, and biggest wins to inspire you on your journey.

In all my personal experiences and the stories I've covered—from natural disasters to the child detention centers on the Southern border, from riots to rallies—I've come to recognize that in every conflict, every tragedy, every overwhelming situation, we are just people with shared humanity, and none of us is perfect. While some things might drive us apart at times, we must try to remember it's our mess, our differences, our struggles large and small, that make us perfectly suited to become the change we want to see in the world.

Closing my eyes now, I remember how that morning with the *GMA* crew ended.

I glanced down at the tan line left by *abuela*'s missing bracelet on my naked wrist. My banged-up feet were outlined by angry red lines where the patent material met my skin. But all of that didn't matter anymore. I was happy, motivated, and immensely grateful to have had the chance of a lifetime. I promised myself that next time I would do better.

¡Cónchale! Yikes! I thought as I walked out of the building. I really wanted a picture of this day, as I often did to commemorate the moments that mark my life.

I waited until a friendly tourist walked by. "Would you mind?" I handed her my iPhone.

As my impromptu photographer tried to get a good shot, she asked if I worked on television. With a burst of enthusiasm, I threw my hands in the air and yelled, "Yes!"

It's been my victory pose ever since.

#Go like Mariana: Embrace what makes you different. You got where you are because of your personality, and that's the only way you will stand out. Take in suggestions respectfully, but try to find your own space without losing your identity.

#Go like Mariana: Defeat the imposter syndrome. Visualize where you started and where you are now. The path forward is carved day by day with sweat, dedication, respect, and a willingness to learn and share what you know.

Count to One Hundred

Caracas, Venezuela, June 2007

I had done the climb up Ávila Mountain at least a hundred times. This Sunday morning wouldn't be any different. When I got back home to my parents' apartment, we'd do what we always did on weekends, eat *arepas*—our traditional tortilla-type sandwich— from my papi's eatery. I was planning to get alterations done for the bridesmaid dress I'd wear to my *amiga*'s wedding and maybe catch one of the Hollywood movies I was obsessed with playing at a nearby theater. (The optimist in me always wants to do a lot more than I actually have time for.)

After changing and brushing my hair into a ponytail, I grabbed my iPod and closed the door behind me.

I was making my way toward the kitchen table to grab my keys when Mami stopped me in my tracks. "*Niña*, are you seriously going to go hiking now?" she asked me as she followed me into the kitchen. "*Tú quieres hacerlo todo*—You want to do everything. You know I need help setting the table since we're expecting your cousins for lunch."

I didn't answer out loud, but I could hear myself mentally bullet-point all the reasons why I needed a break. I knew in my mother's own way she was trying to preserve a degree of normalcy. But the truth was that in Venezuela, my home country, things hadn't been normal in a long time.

After President Hugo Chávez was elected in 1998 on a socialist agenda, his government inched slowly toward what many considered a dictatorship. Following the footsteps of his mentor, Cuba's Fidel Castro, Chávez had been in power for eight years and was changing the constitution so he would be able to reelect himself indefinitely. That month in 2007, he had shut down Radio Caracas Television (RCTV), one of the most important national networks, and replaced it with a state-funded channel. When the signal went black, it was the equivalent of turning off NBC, ABC, or CBS. These actions would spark a wave of student-led protests throughout the year.

I was a junior in college, and I was in the thick of it. My friends would block highways midweek; we made banners and marched all the way downtown. We went to class only to organize; professors would convene meeting points so we could protest together. Peaceful rallies often turned dangerous. Riot police abounded, and they often used tear gas. Violent crime had nearly doubled too. But I knew too much was at stake to stop now. A hike would be good for me—help me clear my mind and sort my priorities. Now standing opposite my mom, I knew this volatile climate was the elephant in the room.

All she ever wants is to keep us safe, I thought.

"I'll be back in time," I assured her, kissed her on the cheek, and went on my way.

The trail began at the foot of Ávila Mountain, a short five-minute walk from the apartment where I grew up. The mountain separates Caracas from the Caribbean Sea. The capital is a city split in two: west Caracas is filled with plastic-sheeting slums and makeshift homes, and east Caracas is full of gated communities and high-rise apartment buildings. In many ways, *El Ávila*, which lies smack in the middle, serves as a refuge of greenery and clean air in the midst of a concrete jungle. In these increasingly polarized times, it's probably one of the last places where Venezuelans from all walks of life can coexist.

The day was glorious. I smiled with excitement just to be out enjoying some version of peace and quiet. *Sí, Mariana, this is just what you needed today,* I told myself.

I could hear the birds chirping along the ascending trail. The cacophony mixed with the sound of tree breeze and food peddlers kept me motivated despite the challenging climb.

Then I spotted a shirtless man out of the corner of my eye. Something about him didn't sit well with me. He had wavy dark hair that was gelled back, with a telenovela-villain look about him. I didn't know why, but I knew it was better to stop and try to lose him.

As I leaned down and pretended to tie my shoelaces, hoping he would continue on his way, he passed me slowly on my right, sizing me up. He nearly brushed against me on the narrow trail, as so many people do while hastily going up and down the mountain. The hairs on my neck stood up. But he disappeared into the next right, and I thought that was over and done with. *Phew, menos mal. Good thinking about those shoelaces!*

The hike took me all the way to a peak overlooking the city. There were other hikers and families around. This peak, called Sabas Nieves, probably offers one of the best views of the valley of Caracas. I stretched out on the ground at the overlook and took it all in. But all the while, I couldn't kick that feeling in the pit of my stomach that someone was watching me.

Ay, Mariana, just shrug it off.

About twenty minutes later, I was slowly making my way down the steep mountain trail when I turned the corner into a shaded area.

Suddenly the shirtless man jumped out from the trees, startling me. As he pounced, predator-like, I saw all his athletic might. His flexed knees almost reached the height of his chest. His arms fully extended toward me. He backed me up against a bush.

Has he been following me all this time? How long had he been hiding, waiting for me?

He pulled out a gun from his shorts and pressed the muzzle against my forehead. His eyes locked with mine. I was paralyzed. "*¡Dame todo lo que tienes!*—Give me everything you've got!"

I only had a fanny pack with an iPod mini that I had ordered in pink for my previous birthday, the equivalent of five dollars, and small gold hoops. (We Latinas have a die-hard habit of not leaving the house without some bling.) Shaking, I handed them over.

Okay, you have everything, I thought. *You can go now . . . Why are you still here?*

We were alone in that stretch of woods. I had no way out. I could see the drops of sweat rolling down his muscles. I also had sweat rolling down my body, from the temperature and from fear.

He showed a hint of a smile. *He was enjoying this.* The mountaintop was so forested, immense, removed. Anything could happen. He could assault me. He could rape me, and no one would see. How would I react? I'd heard resisting makes things worse. What if I never recovered from this?

I couldn't help but kick myself for having left that morning. My mom wanted me to stay back and help. Papi . . . how many times had he begged me to pay attention to my surroundings? And yet here I was in an awful situation that could have been avoided. He prepared me for so many things in life, but back then he couldn't keep my natural disregard for danger in check.

I heard a bird chirping at a distance. My dad had told me he sometimes dreamed of being a bird and often wished to have the power to fly like one. In that critical moment, he was there with me, as always. I felt a little stronger.

Continuing to hold the gun at my forehead, the man commanded me to get on my knees. I dropped and felt the weight of the world go with me. I closed my eyes. *This is it. This is how my story will end. I haven't even done what I wanted to do yet. I am not ready to die!*

"¡Cuenta hasta cien!—Count to one hundred!" he said. I started to count out loud.

The first ten numbers came out fast. Since I didn't hear the sound of his footsteps retreating, I knew he was still there, possibly planning what else to do with this terrified twenty-three-year-old woman who was completely at his mercy.

When my counting reached fifty, I felt the gun—cold and heavy—maliciously sliding down my cheeks and grazing my lips.

"Cincuenta y uno, cincuenta y dos, cincuenta y tres . . ." My mouth trembled so much I didn't even know if I was voicing the numbers correctly.

Crying was not an option. I kept counting, trying to ground myself by pushing my hands into the dirt. *Respira—Just breathe.*

When I finally heard his footsteps receding, I exhaled deeply.

My eyes moved slowly, as if someone else were prying them open. Seeing that I was alone, I got up and started running so fast I almost tripped over tree roots along the path of the steep mountaintop. *He could still be watching me. He could be waiting to follow me home and kill all of us.*

When I got to the bottom, I saw a small guardhouse. Knowing how the police operate in Venezuela, I immediately ditched the idea of reporting what had happened. The robber could be in cahoots with the guards.

I ran for a couple of blocks and stopped in front of my building. I made sure the coast was clear, then grabbed my house keys from the flowerpot and went up to our apartment.

"Mari, are you okay?" both my brother, Alvaro Elias, and sister, Graciela, asked. I looked terrified, and my knees were covered with dirt.

I burst into tears.

The mugging was *la gota que derramó el vaso*, or as they say in English, the straw that broke the camel's back.

After months of escalating political tensions and relentlessly participating with my friends and siblings in student protests against human rights violations by the Venezuelan government, I felt defeated. Things were going to get much worse before they would get better, if they ever did.

That event was a crossroads. Violence forced me to make a decision. As painful as it was, I knew it was time for me to go. I set my sights on the United States. It was the only other country I had spent significant amounts of time in, for camps and summer English courses. If I couldn't be home, I wanted to be in a place that felt at least vaguely familiar and safe.

It would take me more than a decade to realize that the mugging was not only a turning point that propelled me to follow a new path but also a life-changing event that gave me a valuable and unexpected tool.

Now, every time I face a stressful situation that is out of my control, I start slowly counting to one hundred. The numbers set the pace for my ideas and sync up with my heartbeat, which gives me a chance to think and to breathe. I can't get anywhere if I'm not breathing. In particularly nerve-wracking events, counting gives me the chance to remember that to conquer fear, I need to stay calm.

Counting to one hundred takes less than two minutes. That day on the mountain, I could've died before reaching that number. It made me understand that in a matter of moments you can turn your life around, for good or bad. Every minute counts.

That's the thing with trauma. Until you're faced with it, you have no idea how you will react. There isn't a handbook for what to do when someone holds you at gunpoint. When it happened to me, it changed me at my core. The person who hiked up the mountain was not the one who came down. In that moment, I felt I had truly lost the Venezuela of my childhood. The one my parents had worked so hard to fill with safety and fun for our family. The one that felt like a magical place. Now it was falling apart in a much more personal way. Who would I become without my country, the blueprint of my identity?

I would have to make a conscious effort to carry it with me. To take all of it, from beginning to end, good and bad, and let it continue to form me into someone who could survive the storms of the real world. That happy, idealized childhood always had hard truths playing around the edges. To go forward, I would have to go back and face them.

#*Go like Mariana*: Breathe. Count. In frightening or stressful situations, give yourself the gift of a process to help you regain composure and focus on what needs to happen next. It can be as simple as breathing, counting, praying, or having a basic task to fall back on.

#Go like Mariana: Chaos or unwanted situations can drive us to what's next—to something better. How could this be true for you?

2

My Happy Place

La Guaira, Venezuela, 1990

"Kids, get ready. We're going to the beach!" Mami said.

It was music to my six-year-old ears. Every year at the start of the *Carnaval* holiday, as soon as that phrase escaped my mother's lips, joy would resonate throughout the halls of our apartment in the La Castellana neighborhood.

The beach at *Carnaval* felt like the heartbeat of my country. The burlesque processions on the streets, the colorful, exotic birds flying overhead, and the geckos crawling around the sand. The sounds of the ocean, cicadas, and drums. The smells of saltwater, greasy *empanadas de cazón*, and potent *guarapita* (a cocktail of passion fruit, sugarcane, and alcohol). That small part of my vast nation encapsulated the mystery and greatness of my people. It was a reminder of our Latin American magical realism that to this day I find in everything I do. That's where I come from, where I was made.

My family was heading off for a week of fun. *Carnaval* is a typical South American Catholic celebration before Ash Wednesday. Many countries, most famously Brazil, observe this tradition; it is our equivalent to Mardi Gras. Its name comes from the Latin expression *carne levare*, meaning "farewell to meat," or, less literally, to the pleasures of the flesh. For us kids it meant a week of swimming in the Caribbean, lazing under the palm trees, and enjoying almost unlimited freedom. Freedom to run around with our friends in the sand until our legs gave out. Freedom to eat *paletas* (ice lollipops made from fresh fruit) and *tequeños* (our version of mozzarella sticks) any time of day, without supervision, because it was safe enough for us to run around without our parents worrying. It also meant freedom from the limitations of the city of Caracas in the 1990s, where we were constantly constrained.

We couldn't walk or bike outside our apartment. We never got on the bus or subway because it was deemed too dangerous. We were driven everywhere, limiting our relationship with the environment. The beach, however, was the total opposite. We were able to explore it ourselves.

At that time, Venezuela was not the country it is today. In the

1990s, it was still one of the richest nations in South America, a global superpower, and one of the only democracies in a region largely ruled by strongmen. In the 1990s, the Banco de Venezuela had a branch in Manhattan's Upper East Side, which you can see in the background of the Al Pacino film *Scent of a Woman*. It was like having the US Federal Reserve open up a bank in Paris by the Champs-Élysées—that's how influential Venezuela was. Caracas was the first place Dior opened a store outside of the City of Lights. It also attracted immigrants from all over Latin America, Europe, and the Middle East with promises of prosperity. My great-grandfather came from Corsica, a little island off the coast of France. The other side of my family had been in Venezuela since colonial times. They had flourished in Venezuela's economic bonanza for generations.

My siblings and I grew up comfortably in a home with a staff that included a driver, a cook, and a housekeeper. Believe me when I tell you Mami ran our house like Mrs. Hughes from *Downton Abbey*; everything was tidy, we were always on time, and when we traveled, our luggage was packed and waiting for us by the door.

Only a year younger than me, my sister, Graciela, was my other half. We did everything together. Since my mom insisted on dressing us the same, I grew up feeling as if she were an extension of me, and I developed an urge to protect her.

Graciela and I usually got home from school around three in the afternoon, ready to take off our school uniforms. Our knee-high white socks, blue skirts, and button-down shirts had left our house pristinely ironed in the morning only to return wrinkled and smelling of recess and junk food.

On *Carnaval* Friday, we jumped out of the school bus with

more glee than usual. We raced to see who would get to our building's door first, dashing up to the second floor where we lived to hear that liberating phrase: "*Niñitas*—hurry up, girls! We're going to the beach!" We changed as quickly as we could into our beach clothes for the trip.

Our family had inherited a little beach cabin from our grandparents, part of the Club Camurí Grande community in the coastal state of Vargas. Camurí was like one big family, with new guests pouring in every holiday. It had a stream for fishing, two swimming pools, two beaches, a marina, three restaurants, a lighthouse, and a movie theater/church. It was all mixed in with the jungle and sand, in a state of tropical disarray. It wasn't like the organized American lakeside clubs in the Catskills that we see in the movies or in *The Marvelous Mrs. Maisel*.

It was a constant party, with everyone looking to escape the city.

My family would not only spend *Carnaval* there, but also long weekends, some Christmases, and New Year's Eve (when everyone got together to build a big *fogata*, or campfire, on the beach) with plenty to do—surfing, swimming, and Rollerblading. Staying in an enclosed club allowed us to taste the freedom we craved. But it also meant there was a security gate, lifted to give access only to members and guests. A physical barrier to keep away the locals from the nearby shantytowns. But my sister and I were too young to understand all that. It was our happy place, and we loved it there.

Mami usually sent the housekeeper down with the driver a day before to have everything ready for our arrival. They had instructions to turn on the air conditioner and make the beds before leaving to enjoy the holiday with their own families.

Back in those days, the little beach cabins didn't even have phone lines, and there were no cell phones. To communicate with "the capital," you had to go to the beach's central telephone office and make a call.

The cabins were simple two-story houses. They all looked the same from the outside: rustic and off-white with a small open terrace/kitchen that gave way to the lush flora and fauna. Our cabana had two bedrooms: Mami and Papi's and one with bunk beds for us kids.

My sister and I shared a small suitcase. We didn't need much: bathing suits, a pair of flip-flops—which I later begged my mom to switch for the fashionable jelly shoes—and some pajamas. The toys were all at the cabin: pails and shovels, an inflatable zebra and crocodile, and our skates and bikes.

Our days would be spent getting in water balloon fights, making sandcastles, and even making abstract drawings that we later sold to the *abuelos* for the equivalent of a *paleta*, which they happily bought to encourage their grandkids' creativity and entrepreneurial spirit.

Graciela and I started counting down from the moment we got in the car, while Papi loaded the luggage in the back of our blue Toyota Samurai and Mami buckled our baby brother, Alvaro Elias, into the back seat.

Going from the city of Caracas to the coastline required getting to the other side of the Ávila Mountain through a tunnel built in the 1950s. The journey could take anywhere from forty-five minutes to an hour and a half, depending on traffic. It was comparable to leaving New York for the Hamptons on Memorial Day Weekend—with a mango twist.

There was no time to waste, not even to stop and eat. To speed things up, we went by Misia Jacinta, Papi's *arepera* (a cantina-style restaurant), which he proudly ran as a profitable 24-7 business. We grabbed a couple of *arepas* for the road. I secretly wished that one day we would stop by the McDonald's across the street and get a Happy Meal with its sought-after toy, but I didn't want to hurt my dad's feelings.

Arepas, the daily bread of Venezuela, can be opened and stuffed with anything you might fancy that day. They're eaten for breakfast, lunch, or dinner. (That's why my dad's place worked as a 24-7 business.) We loved *arepas* with chicken, avocado, and mayo; shredded chicken and cheddar cheese; or with shredded beef, black beans, and plantains.

In any other family, eating in the car would have been messy, but not under my mom's watch. Mami had paper towels, wipes, and Ziplocs ready to go, and a cooler of Malta sodas to wash the food down.

The first sign that we were outside Caracas and closer to the beach was the fading radio signal. Our ears started popping. The air got dense because of the ocean's humidity. We played at holding our breath until the car crossed the tunnel through the mountains, gasping when we were on the other side.

The foothills revealed a world that was very different from the bubble my parents had created for their kids in the city. It was filled with slums with tin roofs where thousands of impoverished families lived.

At night, when you look at the landscape of Caracas, you see twinkling lights covering the mountain range, like dragonflies

lighting up the sky. But when the sun comes out, the disenchant-
ment hits you like a ton of bricks. It's a favela of millions. Despite
Venezuela's wealth, these marginalized communities suffered from
the severe inequality that reigned there. Addressing that disparity
and social injustice was a central tenet of the campaign platform
that made Colonel Hugo Chávez president in 1998.

By the time he took office, he inherited a country where many
Venezuelans' wages were nearly 70 percent below what they had
been during the huge oil boom twenty years prior. Despite the
prosperity my home country enjoyed, the truth is that corruption,
collusion, and poor policies made it impossible to close the painful
gap that would end up tearing us apart. It's why so many went
hungry while others did not.

My school, Merici Academy, opened my eyes to the gulf between
rich and poor in our communities. I attended this school, run by
Ursuline nuns, all fourteen years of my primary and lower sec-
ondary education. The motto embroidered on our uniform was
Serviam (in Latin, "I will serve").

Merici funded a school for underprivileged kids ironically called
Campo Rico, or "Rich Field," financed by our families' donations.
Once a year, the children would come spend the day with us, and
the contrasts became even more startling.

I'll never forget how their eyes lit up at the sight of our school
supplies, our shoes, and even the pretty bows on our neatly brushed
hair. To them, some of us looked like real-life princesses.

Even at my young age, I knew something was wrong. Mami

worked part-time in the Salvation Army–type donation center for *Campo Rico* for ten years. Our parents financed their school and welcomed students to our facilities for a day. But we didn't really befriend them. We didn't know their names or the travails they experienced at home. We weren't doing enough.

Now I know that to actually help those in need, we have to go further than paying for their basic education or showing them there is a better world out there. We have to give them tools as individuals and as a community so they can fight for their dreams, and we have to motivate them to believe in themselves, to recognize their potential. Today *Serviam* means, to me, that I will do everything within my power to encourage the personal and professional growth of the people in my path, to reach across the painful gaps that separate us, no matter what they are; gaps that I failed to notice as a kid on our trips to the beach.

As we drove through a small shantytown called Naiguatá just before reaching the beach club, I used to press my face against the window with curiosity. I saw kids running barefoot across the road and heard the sound of salsa music flooding the back alleys. Women in thongs selling kisses (and probably everything else) for a couple of *bolívares*, our local currency. Street vendors offered *coquitos*— South American eggnog—and every other alcoholic drink you can imagine. Plenty of ruckus to distract me from the signs of poverty. I often looked at kids who were my age or younger in amazement. All of them seemed to do whatever they pleased with big smiles. At least that's what I thought.

Once we reached the beach club, our own feeling of freedom started to kick in.

We ran into the ocean without a worry. We didn't even have to think about money. Back then, at Club Camurí, we would each get a little booklet of fake Monopoly-style cash we could use for soda, candy, or even supplies at the bodega.

Every year the club members threw a beach party and invited a local music group called *Las Sardinas de Naiguatá*—the Sardines of Naiguatá—to play. These fishermen by trade but musicians at heart came with their drums, Caribbean tambourines, and the *Carnaval* queen. Decked out in colorful shirts and painted faces, they played a unique mixture of Venezuelan and Dominican merengue, combined with the rhythm of African drums that runs through our veins. The party was a procession of hundreds of people dancing and taking over the street that led to the club's entrance. Some dressed in drag while others wore elaborate costumes with their faces painted; there was alcohol galore, and everyone marched to the music. The queen presided over it all.

I was eight years old the first time I really noticed the woman who wore the crown—with her caramel skin, luscious, glossy lips, and a necklace of wildflowers. That year's queen, unlike the city queens, had a simple costume—a white, one-shouldered dress, almost Grecian. She didn't need any additional embellishment. Her exuberance was plenty. I'd never seen a beauty like hers.

I should say that in Venezuela, beauty is the country's second export. It is one of the few things that offers women a chance at upward mobility. It's so enmeshed in our culture that we elect beauty queens for everything, including baseball, soccer, and basketball teams. There are beauty queens in village holidays, harvests, companies, in grade schools, and even in prisons—"The most beautiful convict."

It's also very telling of the huge gender gap and inherent racism. In a country where a majority of the population is mestizo, of mixed indigenous and European origin, many of the *misses*, or queens, are usually white, tall blondes or very light brunettes.

But as soon as she came to Club Camurí with the local band for the festivities, I saw that the Queen of Naiguatá was different. She looked at me briefly and smiled. She wasn't cold or distant, with a frozen smile like the ones on TV. She was strong and majestic, with her tanned skin, curly hair, and musical laugh.

I was a short, hairy little girl who showed her gums when she smiled, but suddenly the possibility of transforming from an ugly duckling into a swan became real to me. It was like a revelation. This woman was perfectly, authentically herself.

If by any stroke of luck I could feel as confident and safe in my own skin as she was, I wouldn't need to compare myself to the other girls in their elaborate costumes who body-shamed those of us who didn't fit our society's standards of beauty.

I was so inspired by her that I decided to participate in the club's costume competition. It was for kids, but it was serious business. The contestants' parents put a lot of thought into choosing the outfits and accessories. Kids would walk a white runway set in the middle of the club's tropical garden and compete with other children their age.

With a necklace of wildflowers and my best smile, I withstood the snarky comments from the other girls who called me tacky for emulating the village queen. I got on that catwalk with pride and even danced to the drums without caring whether I jived with the beat or not. In the end, to everyone's surprise, I won!

It would take me decades to deconstruct that event. It took a lot of inner growth before I could truly accept myself for who I am. Now my smile comes from within, my confidence is genuine, and I respect the fact that my petite body is strong, healthy, and takes me around the world doing the job I love.

I wish I could go back and thank that young woman who unknowingly became one of my first female role models. Her image lives in me. Her spontaneity still moves me, and the memory of the light in her eyes, which locked on mine for only a couple of seconds, gives me strength when any negative comments threaten to open the Pandora's box of my fears and self-doubt.

Our backgrounds were starkly different, but *la Reina de Naiguatá* taught me that the human spirit soars over those barriers. Bringing our real selves forward is far more powerful than cultivating mere beauty or meeting a checklist of expectations, and it can bring freedom to others in ways more powerful than we might realize.

At the beach club, my parents sat by the rocks in the same spot every morning, year after year. They would set up plastic green chairs alongside their group of friends on a stretch of sand we referred to as "the elders' beach," because the younger crowd didn't hang out there. My siblings and I showed up only at lunchtime to let our folks know we were safe and sound.

At night, an improvised movie theater in the church auditorium was the place to be. They would set up a giant projector in the same space where mass was held on Sundays, walls open on the sides so you could hear the ocean. My fascination with Hollywood and my desire to learn English started in that little auditorium.

I would sit there starry-eyed, night after night, watching movies like *Top Gun* and *Home Alone*, whose star, Macaulay Culkin, I fell in love with as a twelve-year-old girl. I strived to imitate everything he did in the film. I made several attempts at placing toy cars on the floor so my math teacher would slip and fall like the robbers, and I even tried to throw myself on a zip line made with a clothes hanger from the second floor of our apartment like Macaulay did to get to his tree house. Thankfully, my mom stopped me before I jumped out—and the next thing I knew, she had metal bars installed in our bedroom window.

I also cried for days after watching Macaulay in *My Girl*, where his character dies from bee stings sustained while looking for the mood ring his beloved friend Vada had lost. Honestly, who thought up such a cruel movie? On top of a distinct dislike for bees, I developed a strong urge to have my first kiss "before dying," just like Macaulay's character did.

The opportunity came about some years later. I had set my heart on a boy who was slightly older than me. His name was Reinaldo Herrera. He was elegant, like an English lord straight from the movies I so admired. His aunt was fashion designer Carolina Herrera, so he came by his style naturally. But besides his looks, he had something special. Reinaldo had the maturity of a gentleman, and he behaved the same with or without adult supervision. He was noble. Honest. Good. When he smiled I felt the rest of the world vanish.

One year, on the last night of *Carnaval*, I noticed him by the lighthouse. He was alone, looking up at the stars.

I said to myself, *Okay, Mariana . . . just start walking up to him. You can do it. God, please let him like me.* I felt my heart ready to burst out of my chest. But somehow I found the courage to talk to him.

"*Hola*, Rey . . . um . . . I need to tell you something important." He looked at me, wide-eyed.

"I want to kiss you before I die!" I blurted out with my melodramatic teen voice, eyes twinkling with curiosity about something I had only seen in movies and telenovelas.

My prayers must have worked, because he got up and held my face in his hands with infinite tenderness.

"Are you sure?" he asked.

I barely managed to nod with a silent but definite yes.

His lips slowly rested on mine like the wings of a butterfly, subtle but unforgettable. That night, under the stars, I became his girlfriend.

Reinaldo was a very shy, conservative guy—a sweetheart, a gentleman. We dated all through our high school years, but we didn't share the same adventurous spirit. After some years I realized that perfect as he was, I wasn't going to be able to be "perfectly me" with him. Even though we went our separate ways, I took with me the memory of those magical beach days, lit by the passion of *Carnaval*.

The closing ritual to mark the end of *Carnaval* is called the Burial of the Sardine, celebrated on Ash Wednesday. We watched as the townspeople participated in a mock-funeral procession. It's like a block party; people dance and cry to the music as they march to the beat of the drums. Ladies dressed in black dramatically wail and dab their eyes with handkerchiefs. "Mourners" in over-the-top costumes and pallbearers carry the dear-departed "sardine" with great ceremony to the place where it will be eulogized.

The giant sardine—made of cardboard, the size of a person—represents the sinful desires of the flesh and is papered over with "salacious" photos and newspapers. The procession is led by a fake priest and altar boys and accompanied by a crowd of hundreds. Starting in the fishing docks, they make their way through the masses while people throw fake holy water at each other (taken from coolers with actual rum), calling for lusts to be purged.

When they reach their destination, the widows—a group of men in drag—cry over the body of the sardine to the rhythm of the tambourine, the *cuatro* (a small guitar), and the drums of the town band, the Sardines of Naiguatá. They carry palms in their hands to shoo away flies, witches, and demons. By nightfall, the sardine is thrown back into the sea to be with the real fish while the procession mourns. This closes the cycle, marking the end of the holiday.

Looking back at it now, I love how the colors, sounds, and smells are a distillation of my culture, with an idiosyncrasy that is characteristically mestizo, full of flavor and fast-talkin' Spanish you'd recognize anywhere you see a Venezuelan. It became an indelible part of who I am. This was the joyful place of my youth, albeit one of deep divides. I didn't know then that it would all vanish one day without warning.

On December 15, 1999, a monumental landslide caused by heavy rains hit Venezuela. It pummeled coastal areas in the state of Vargas, killing thousands of people in the shantytowns where they lived in the illegal *ranchos*, which were known to be a health hazard. At that time about 80 percent of the population of Caracas was impoverished, and the only affordable places to live were in the outskirts of the mountains near the city.

Trees, debris, and soil began to move down the hills. Then came a torrential downpour that lasted for days. A massive movement of rocks tumbled down the slopes. The roads and towns in its wake, including Naiguatá, were completely blocked off and destroyed.

My sister and I were in the capital that day. But my parents and Alvaro Elias were at the beach club. Then in our teens, Graciela and I had decided to stay home and study for final exams. That night, though, we couldn't sleep and stayed up watching the news of the rains and the damage in the area. At eight o'clock the next morning, we finally got ahold of our family through the central telephone office and warned them to get out as fast as possible. They managed to get on the road, but the flash floods were sucking away everything in their path.

Club Camurí's small dam collapsed. The streets and dirt roads where I had bounced along as a child turned into perilous rivers.

My mom remembers looking back and watching the water and

mud violently breaching the cabins. They tried to get out, but they couldn't get any farther than the next town over. Everyone was trying to escape, and traffic blocked the roads. Some got stuck in the mud, which eventually turned into quicksand.

As they began to turn back, my brother noticed the surge coming toward their car. Water leaked in above the wheels and almost through the doors.

"I could feel the earth tremble and vibrate," he later told me. "It was like an earthquake, the houses and rocks atop the mountains falling like dominoes while the ocean turned dark red from the mud."

"Papi, go, go, go—hit the gas pedal, go now!" my brother yelled as my dad tried to steer the car out of the dirt. They couldn't return to Camurí, so they sought refuge at a friend's apartment building nearby, where they waited on the balcony of the seventh floor because the lower levels were completely immersed in water. The torrent was so close, once they reached the building and looked down, the whole street they had driven on was flooded.

In Caracas, my sister and I lived moments of desperation without knowing where my parents and brother were. We prayed every hour. I fervently asked God to save my family. The images on TV were devastating. We knew they had left the club, but we didn't know what had become of them until almost midnight, when they were able to call.

Three days later, a chopper rescued the people in their building, and they returned to us.

Thousands weren't as lucky. According to estimates, the landslide of Vargas took the lives of ten thousand to thirty thousand people, 10 percent of the state's population. Almost three hundred thousand people were affected by the Vargas tragedy, featured in the Guinness Book of World Records as the mudslide with the highest death toll. This tragedy touched the lives of rich and poor alike: people in the enclosed fancy beach clubs, the small villages, and the shantytowns like Naiguatá.

What nature did, man worsened. The catastrophe further exposed the division between groups, as some of the poorest people saw it as a chance to break into the clubs and loot. Wealthier residents, meanwhile, retreated into the city and didn't help villages like Naiguatá recover. Thousands of displaced people were taken to an improvised shelter in a huge stadium in the capital and forgotten about, as though they were garbage that needed to be disposed of. They eventually got fed up and left; most would never be able to return home.

These small cities turned into places you pass by quickly in a bulletproof car. That part of La Guaira never recovered its former splendor.

Entire neighborhoods disappeared as a result of the floods. Hotels and small businesses were simply erased. The lush jungle-like foliage turned brown and brittle. The sand devoured the coastline until the beach was unrecognizable.

The landscape changed entirely. And whatever the floods didn't destroy, the looters took with them. Decades of inequality busted at the seams in those December days, some of the most painful in our country's history.

I still remember a close friend of my mom's saying, "I wish the rains would have washed away the shantytowns and all those people who lived there." Horrified, my mom promptly told her to leave our house and go talk to a priest about these thoughts. Racism, bigotry, hypocrisy, and prejudice were everywhere, but I didn't know what to say or do. I felt so frustrated and powerless. What could we do as individuals to heal these deep wounds? How could a country have a sense of unity if some of its citizens showed such disregard for the lives of others?

Now, when I cover natural disasters, manmade suffering, or political unrest, I feel there's finally something I can do. I know it's my responsibility not only to show the aftermath of a hurricane, a mass shooting, an earthquake, or a fatal accident, but to reveal the true dimension of its human loss. To come back a year or five years later and make viewers remember the faces beyond the headlines, from Ferguson, Haiti, and the Charleston church shooting, to Hurricane Maria in Puerto Rico or Mexico's earthquake.

I try to cover these tragedies in a way that reflects that we are all human—that we all deserve a chance to have a good life and thrive. I take La Guaira with me every time I cover a new story. A happy place can fall apart in what seems like an instant. Despite our best efforts to protect ourselves, life happens—over and over again. Divisions can grow slowly, without us realizing their full implications. We can't recover from any of this without remembering where we all came from—and how much we have in common.

#Go like Mariana: Bringing our real selves to the table is far more powerful than cultivating mere beauty or meeting a checklist of expectations. It can bring freedom to others in ways more powerful than we might realize.

#*Go like Mariana*: If people throughout history would have been more in tune with their peers and found ways to understand and cooperate with one another, perhaps we wouldn't have to learn so many war stories in school. Along with being empathetic and respectful, we need to make a conscious effort to give those in need the tools to achieve their dreams.

3

"Please Don't Look Too Latina"

Minnesota, 1993

One day when I was around seven years old, my dad told me, "Mariana, I'm going to send you along with your sister to a place where nobody speaks Spanish. I want you to experience different cultures."

He kept going on about the benefits of spending an entire summer in the United States, stressing a little phrase I didn't pay much attention to at the time: "You never know what the future holds."

Meanwhile, I thought, *Maybe I'll get to go to camp in Miami! Even better, maybe I'll go a little farther north where Mickey Mouse lives!*

My dad had a slightly different plan.

From Caracas, he sent us to a summer camp in Brainerd, Minnesota.

Let's just say that Mickey Mouse wasn't up there.

Mind you, this was before cell phones, Instagram, and Snapchat, so I couldn't look up any information on the place where we were going.

When we got there, I noticed that most of the other kids' hair was several shades of blond and the majority had blue or green eyes.

We looked like we came out of *The Jungle Book* or *Aladdin*.

On the first night, the director gathered everyone around the campfire and said, "Kids, this year we have a very international camp. The Atencios are here from Venezuela."

The other kids didn't know where my country was. They would ask, "Do you know what a hamburger is?" Or, "Do you go to school on a donkey or a canoe?" In my broken English I would try to answer, and they would just laugh.

They were probably not trying to be mean; they just wanted to understand who we were and make a correlation with the world they knew. For them the world was divided into two groups: those who were like them and those who were like characters in a book filled with adventures.

We were "different." And as a little kid, that hurt. But being the oldest, it was my responsibility to make my sister feel safe, so I put on my brave face and decided to learn everything I could about the American way of life.

We did what we later called the "Summer Experience" for eight years. During that time, my younger siblings and I would finish the school year in Venezuela and then go off to learn English in a series of US towns that I can proudly say not many Americans know as well as we do.

Afterward, we would come back home and keep up with our second language by watching a little TV set in our living room that picked up the American networks, where I later discovered newswomen like Katie Couric, Diane Sawyer, Andrea Mitchell, and Christiane Amanpour.

No matter how much our English improved, clicking with someone in a foreign country year after year wasn't easy. Making a friend was like a special reward, and through those years I made some that I still keep in touch with.

The truth is, we all need to feel valued and accepted. We think it should happen spontaneously, but it doesn't. When you are different, as we were, you have to work at belonging. You might feel you have to be really nice or extremely smart, good-looking, helpful, funny—anything to be "cool" for the crowd you want to hang out with. Sometimes you end up choosing to change who you are in order to please others. And sometimes that follows you into adulthood. Those childhood experiences can hang on much longer than you'd think.

Miami, 2017

As much as we care about what people think of us when we're young, as adults, saying that we don't care at all about other people's opinions is just not true. As part of any society we have to build relationships with friends, colleagues, and even with family members that will be framed and defined by what they think of us and what we think of them. And like it or not, people often base their opinions on the way we look.

Discussing a female journalist's appearance is commonplace on TV. For those of us in front of the camera, it can feel like a beauty pageant that no one signed up for. Our peers and supervisors make comments that can immediately impact our careers and self-esteem.

Why did she pick a sleeveless shirt?

She looks like a million bucks today!

Need we say more?

One of the first questions I get asked by almost everyone when I'm invited to appear at an event, even if it's a speaking engagement, is "What are you going to wear?"

I know it sounds superficial, but in many industries women are still expected to fit into a certain mold if they want to be taken seriously. Well, if people are going to make this into a beauty pageant, I want to wear a band across my body that says, *Mi Gente!*

After a decade working in media, and having crossed over from Univision to MSNBC, I have gotten used to comments about my looks. But instead of fretting over people's judgment of my appearance, I have learned to take back my power and use dress as a subtle way of telling people, "I'm here—and I'm not pretending to be someone else. Guess what? You can be whatever you want without changing your essence."

So you can imagine my delight when I found out I was going to the White House Correspondents' Dinner in the spring of 2017. Hosted by the White House Correspondents' Association, the dinner, or nerd prom as it is affectionately called, is the most high-profile media event of the year, traditionally attended by the president and covered by the news media. It was a great opportunity to let my looks reflect who I am.

I had already attended once before during Barack Obama's tenure, in 2014, representing Univision and Fusion, and I was mesmerized by the glitz and glamour. Besides getting to see the president and first lady Michelle Obama, I had spotted so many Hollywood stars it was hard to keep track. I saw the cast of *Scandal, House of Cards, The Good Wife,* and *Modern Family,* along with celebrated comedians, news anchors, reporters, and documentary filmmakers.

They had all been mingling about the dinner tables, like at your cousin's wedding, much more accessible than they would be at a red-carpet Hollywood event. In my opinion, the White House Correspondents' Dinner puts many galas in Tinseltown to shame.

But that first time, I noticed there weren't many Latinos present—simply because there aren't that many Latinos in national news media to begin with. Yet, according to the Census Bureau, Latinos are the largest minority in the US and by 2060 will comprise about 30 percent of the total population, around 119 million.

So, when NBC invited me to go to nerd prom in 2017 as part of their team, I was thrilled to represent our people, proud of having a seat at the table, literally and figuratively. I wanted to make a small tribute to my heritage. I had an idea—what if I wore something yellow, blue, and red, the flag colors of so many South American nations?

I chose a Sofia Vergara–style mermaid gown with yellowish undertones, big royal blue earrings, and a red clutch. *¡Perfecto!*

Bags packed and ready by the door, I was whipping up a quick pre-flight lunch with my husband when my cell phone rang. It was one of the female managers at the network.

"Mariana, I just wanted to make sure you're prepared for such a prestigious gathering," the person said. "What are you going to wear?"

It was a weird phone call—with an even weirder request.

"Why do you ask?" I replied.

"Please don't look too Latina."

At first I thought I didn't hear correctly. "I beg your pardon?" I asked.

"When you pick your outfit, I mean. Don't look too Latina."

I felt offended. Outrage and indignation hit me at once.

"Um, I'm sorry—what does that even mean?" I asked as my voice started trembling from the humiliation.

This person was making me feel smaller and smaller with each word.

Can you imagine someone in your field asking you to please not look so African American? Or Asian? Or white? Don't look so Muslim or Christian? How do you change who you are?

"I still don't understand what I am supposed to do or not do," I said, trying to grasp what was really happening.

"Why don't you go to Saks Fifth Avenue and have someone help you out?" was the next suggestion. (I didn't feel like mentioning that I'd had a personal shopper at Saks since I was at Univision.) "Have them pick out something demure. Not too colorful or tight. Think Ivanka Trump, okay? Let me know if you run into any trouble. Bye."

I thought about the multicolored outfit I'd already packed.

My self-esteem. My identity. Even my community had taken a beating in my mind. What's worse is that this reaffirmed the belief that there is a formula to how people should look. For a moment, I felt like I was back at summer camp, feeling different and out of place.

I am a fair-skinned, straight-haired, freckly Latina. Back home, I was considered white because of my European ancestry and socio-economic status.

I can't change my genetic makeup or the family I was born into, but I am painfully aware that it gives me a degree of privilege. In the United States that usually means I'm not followed in a store and police officers don't ask me if I have a green card when they hear me speaking in Spanish. It also means my education level doesn't get questioned, while other Latinos are constantly on the receiving end of senseless racial profiling and prejudice based on the color of their skin.

This is textbook colorism, which was defined by Alice Walker in her book *In Search of Our Mothers' Gardens* as the "prejudicial or preferential treatment of same-race people based on their color."

In the US, colorism can be traced back to slavery, when lighter-skinned servants would work in the home instead of in the fields. Colorism was also a huge part of Spanish Colonialism that permeates Latin American culture.

Some in our community still judge people as too white or too brown, not white enough or not brown enough, so there is never a way to satisfy everyone.

"Enough!" I wanted to scream into that phone. I wish I could tell you I thought up a clever and cutting reply. But, shocked, I hung up and remained silent.

My husband noticed my watery eyes.

"Jose. I was just told not to look too Latina! What does that even mean?" I asked as he hugged me tightly. "Does it mean don't dress like JLo, Selena Gomez, or Salma Hayek? Because I am sure 99 percent of women in the world would want to look like them!"

Ugh. That's exactly what I should have said.

Then my husband, who is your typical engineer—a man of science, if you will, and not as passionate when it comes to talking about identity as I am—proceeded to confess something equally hurtful that had happened to him.

"I'm sorry, Mari, *lo siento mucho*. I can understand how you must be feeling because sometimes I've felt like that too when dealing with my work," he admitted.

Jose is an MIT grad who came to the US from Venezuela around the same time I did to fulfill his dream of opening a successful business. His family on his father's side is Lebanese, with a history of generational migration. There are more Lebanese living outside the country (eight to fourteen million) than within (four million). His family has had to migrate twice, from Lebanon and most recently from Venezuela.

After working at McKinsey and Company as a consultant for years, Jose had managed to save enough money to launch his startup in South Florida, one that involved his biggest passion: golf. After six years, TheGrint, his app for golfers that calculates a player's free handicap, was called "a game changer" for the sport by CNN Big Ideas, making golf more accessible to younger and more diverse enthusiasts.

But Jose says it's still a very "white" sport, no matter how many championships Tiger Woods or other minority players may have won.

"I've had to change the signature on my email to get investors and users to respond fairly and quickly," he told me that day in our kitchen. "I noticed that when I signed off as 'Jose Torbay,' I got dismissed or ignored. But when I signed off with my initials, JT, I got more responses," he explained.

"For some reason, even when people read my name next to the initials CEO, I am sometimes still viewed as Jose the gardener, not Jose the MIT entrepreneur," he said. "Today you were viewed as Mariana the housekeeper, not the national correspondent."

There are nearly fifty-eight million Hispanics in the US. Some are gardeners and housekeepers; some are fruit pickers or waiters. They do good, essential work, and we should all be proud of them and thankful for what they do. Unfortunately, the stereotypes plaguing Latinos—in Hollywood, in the news media, and in politics—prevent us from being seen as doctors, lawyers, astronauts, and CEOs. Stereotypes grow dangerous when, instead of being considered part of the vital workforce, we are all lumped in with the worst of society—gang members, rapists, criminals.

My husband and I—both hardworking Latino Millennials and legal immigrants—were experiencing just a fraction of the devastating consequences of a wave of intolerance that started to engulf the US in 2016.

In years past, I had perceived it in small things that made me feel like an outsider, such as when I was little and we first started the "Summer Experience" in the US. As I got older, there was the time someone yelled, "We speak English here—welcome to America!" when they overheard me talking in Spanish at the nail salon. Once a work colleague asked, "Are you finally going to marry an American?" and when I answered, "My fiancé is actually Lebanese-Venezuelan," they replied, "You might as well join ISIS. Ha!"

It's not funny. But you simply let it slide most of the time because it takes courage and a tremendous amount of energy to confront racism and xenophobia.

Fast-forward to the thirty-three-year-old correspondent who had just been called out before a black-tie event with a warning to avoid looking "too Latina." I felt again like a seven-year-old kid from South America trying to fit in, which is probably why I didn't dare say anything.

I yielded, calling my stylist at Saks and picking up a "safer" option on my way to the airport. The fact that I didn't stand up for myself revealed a weakness. And that got me thinking about times when I had remained silent and also about moments when I had made *others* feel bad for being different.

Connecticut, 2002

I was finishing high school in Venezuela when my parents sent me to a boarding school in Wallingford, Connecticut, for my senior year. My active imagination had me dreaming of an American high school experience with a locker that looked just like the ones in my favorite TV show at the time, *Saved by the Bell*.

When I got to my dorm, they told me my assigned roommate was eagerly waiting. I opened the door, and there she was, sitting on her bed. With a headscarf! She was Muslim. Her name was Fatima, and she was from Bahrain. She was not what I expected. She must have sensed my disappointment. Honestly, I didn't do much to hide it.

As a teenager I just wanted to be popular, maybe have a boyfriend to go to prom with. I thought that Fatima, with her shyness and strict dress code, would be a hurdle for any relationship I wished to have.

I couldn't understand why she had to pray five times a day or why we couldn't have boys come over if she wasn't wearing her headscarf. I didn't see that I was making her feel the way the kids at summer camp made me feel. My lack of empathy was the equivalent of me asking her, "Do you know what a hamburger is?"

I was consumed by my own selfishness and unable to put myself in her shoes. At that point in my life, I failed to see her as an exceptional and interesting human being.

We lasted only a couple of months together. She was transferred to another dorm where she shared a room with a counselor instead of other students. *That's best for her. She'll be okay; she's just different,* I told myself.

When we label people as different, they become "the other," and it dehumanizes them. They are not worthy of our time, not our problem. In fact, they could even be the cause of our problems in our minds.

So how do we acknowledge our blind spots? First, by understanding what makes us different in someone else's eyes and embracing those traits. When we are comfortable with ourselves, we become ready to appreciate what makes others special.

That truth hit me a couple of months later. I had made new friends, found that date for prom, and almost forgotten about Fatima, until I signed on to participate in a talent show to raise money for charity. Every participant had to offer something for auction. Everybody seemed to have a worthy talent. Some played the violin; others did theater monologues.

I kept thinking, *We don't practice talents like that back home.* But I was determined to come up with something valuable.

The day of the show came, and it was my turn. I got up on stage with a little boom box and played a hit song by my favorite emerging artist at the time: Shakira. "Whenever, wherever . . . we are meant to be together."

I said, "My name is Mariana, and I'm going to auction off a dance lesson."

It seemed as if the whole school raised their hands to bid. My dance class must have stood out from the tenth violin class auctioned that day!

As I walked back to my dorm, I didn't feel different. I felt special! And then I started thinking about Fatima. I realized she was from the Middle East, like Shakira's family, and maybe could have taught me a thing or two about their style of dancing or their beautiful traditions, had I been open to it.

Embracing my differences helped me start embracing others'. We may feel guarded or ashamed of what makes us different, or suspicious of the things that make *other* people different. But those differences could be our best assets. We have so much to offer each other.

I never did apologize to Fatima, which is something I regret to this day.

When I got back home to Venezuela after my year abroad, I began to feel how these experiences were changing me. Being perceived as different made me less judgmental. Empathy is a skill that can be worked on. It can also be learned. And if something can be learned, then there is hope we can change for the better. That notion became one of the reasons I went into journalism.

In 2017, during that White House Correspondents' event, I wore the Ivanka-type gown that had been suggested. Even though I smiled for the cameras, I was miserable.

I finally understood my purpose wasn't just about getting my dream job at a TV network; my real mission would be trying to change the game from within. Showing those young girls with names that are hard to pronounce that they, too, can make it, whatever that means to each one of them, by staying true to themselves.

Miami, 2017

The media has the power to establish the nation's agenda. Journalists determine what the headlines will be. And when you have diverse voices in the newsroom, the coverage reflects a more inclusive news landscape.

Diversity in the stories is important, but so is the authenticity of the storytellers. Organizations need to nurture an environment where new voices aren't morphed into existing ones but become empowered to speak up with their own perspectives, their own cultural flavor, and their own words. We don't need the next so-and-so; we need the new, original emerging figures who will keep moving our profession forward.

And even though something like a dress might seem small, it can be meaningful—in a good or bad way. I still think back to that awkward phone conversation as a missed opportunity. I regret not having brought this up immediately after the fact. Perhaps, if I had voiced how this made me feel, this person would have understood. The ripple effect of little things can be extraordinary.

Sometimes it starts with something like pronouncing our names correctly. Remember *Maria, Marinara*? Well, my parents named me *Mariana*, and I want to honor the way they intended it to sound. I think it's our responsibility—especially if we work on TV or radio—to try to respect the cadence and rhythm of words in their native tongues. I have seen several *Johns* bothered by being called *Yon* in Spanish. I understand how frustrating that is, as much as I understand that it's difficult to roll the *r* in Spanish or even in French, but let's not make fun of it. If you notice, we use words and phrases in other languages all the time. Some have become so frequent that we don't even think about them as foreign, like *chic*, *bon appétit*, or *quesadilla*.

Along with language there are more subtle ways to celebrate our heritage.

When Congresswoman Ilhan Omar proudly wears her hijab or Supreme Court Justice Sonia Sotomayor and Congresswoman Alexandria Ocasio-Cortez display their hoops and red lips, they are sending a powerful message to the world, turning little ripples into bigger waves and then larger representation icons.

One of the best lessons I've learned is that we can't keep preaching to the choir. We Latinos need to find allies in other communities, in our neighborhoods and workplaces. On the small screen it's been people like Joy Reid, Ali Velshi, or Mika Brzezinski who have given me their support and advice on how to cover Latino issues based on their own experiences.

Latinos (or Latinx, as this generation refers to our community to include any gender and other types of diversity) are hardworking, strong, happy, loyal, family oriented, colorful, kind, and vibrant. We come in all shapes, sizes, colors, and accents. But whenever any of us migrate to the United States, no matter where we have come from, whether we eat *empanadas, tamales,* or *arepas,* whether we dance *salsa, cumbia,* or *norteño,* we all become part of the greater Latino community in the United States.

"As soon as you cross the border, you are Latino." That was one of the most powerful things I ever heard from Mario Kreutzberger Blumenfeld, better known by his stage name Don Francisco, the host of *Sábado Gigante,* the longest-running variety series in television history worldwide, which ended in 2015 with fifty-three seasons.

It took a lot of soul searching to fully understand the impact of what Don Francisco said to me. When I left my home country, I knew who I was: a Venezuelan. And while I had seen and read about Latino identity, it was definitely a foreign concept to me when I grew up in Caracas. It wasn't until I came here that I truly began my reeducation process.

As an immigrant, I embraced a more complex definition. Often I was confronted with some upsetting comments like "You're a 'white Latina'" or "Your accent is not too heavy."

Sometimes those comments were meant as compliments, but I felt they were condescending. It gets old telling people that Latinos come in all ethnic types. One cannot look "more" or "less" Latina, whatever that means.

Having an accent, on the other hand, could be something to work on, but it also means that you have the ability to communicate in different languages. Obviously, as a television journalist it is important for me to speak as clearly as possible. But accents should be worn like a medal. I do not want to lose mine. I do not want to dress like everyone else. I do not want to blend in. I want my voice to sound like who I am now: a Latina immigrant, working hard for her dreams, finding her space in this great nation, without ever forgetting where she came from. I will make no apologies for looking the way I do or talking the way I talk or defending my beliefs.

Now, in the twenty-first century, what defines a Latinx person, especially here in the United States, is our shared cultural identity—not a skin tone, not the ability to speak Spanish. We are very comfortable calling our kids Salma, Hans, Katsumi, Kenya, or Jennifer, along with José, Ana, Eva, or Guillermo.

Latino identity is also a melting pot. And we need to understand what ties us together, what divides us, and what makes us weak or strong. That knowledge should be used to make us grow, to help us understand each other's struggles, to be kind to our own and to others, instead of letting it become another form of division.

We can't choose what we look like or where we come from, if we were born in a fancy hospital or a community clinic. But every person gets to choose how to use the power each one of us has, big or small, to help our cause. We need to celebrate our differences and make them building blocks, not rocks to throw at each other.

When I cover stories about immigration, people often ask my position on this issue, and all I tell them is that I am an immigrant, who almost became undocumented when I lost my job (more on that later). One day I was suddenly in danger of becoming *illegal*, a derogatory term that should never be applied to a person.

Thankfully, I managed to avoid a possible deportation by enrolling in school, with the help of my family. Not a lot of people have that luxury. Still, it took a lot of hard work to go from being unemployed and almost undocumented to working at a mainstream national network, and making it to their table at the White House Correspondents' Dinner.

Sitting there, I thought of many Latinos who have really fought for our community. Historical icons like Cesar Chavez and Dolores Huerta, American labor leaders and civil rights activists who founded the United Farm Workers Union to ensure workers their rights in the 1960s. Their nonviolent methods made the farm workers' struggle a moral cause with a national platform, symbolizing Hispanic empowerment based on grassroots organizing.

After Cesar Chavez's death, many schools, parks, and streets were named in his honor. Dolores Huerta is almost ninety and still fighting. She received the Presidential Medal of Freedom and was the first Latina inducted into the National Women's Hall of Fame in 1993. She is also known for coming up with the slogan "*Si, se puede*" ("Yes, we can"), later adopted by Barack Obama for his 2008 campaign.

From organizing the Delano Grape Strike in 1965 in California, where she was the lead negotiator in getting Hispanic workers better conditions in their contracts, to protecting DREAMers, denouncing family separations, and canvassing to get people to vote in 2018, Dolores is still living up to that slogan "*Si se puede*."

We have come a long way since the 1960s. The Congressional

Hispanic Caucus has more Latino elected officials than ever in history. Latinos in the mainstream may have reached an inflection point, with Sonia Sotomayor making history as the first Latina Supreme Court justice; Sofia Vergara being the highest-paid TV actress in 2016; Maria Hinojosa becoming the first Latina to anchor a *Frontline* report on PBS and helping to launch *LatinoUSA* (one of the earliest public radio programs devoted to the Latino community); Lin Manuel Miranda teaching us a lesson on the Founding Fathers and the value of immigration with Broadway's *Hamilton*; and the phenomenal success of Luis Fonsi's "Despacito" remix co-written by Panamanian composer Erika Ender, featuring Justin Bieber, the lyrics of which are mostly in Spanish.

But it's not enough. Our power still doesn't reflect the power of our numbers. We have to keep going; we can't compromise an inch. And it starts with each one of us. It starts with little things we still confront every day, like that phone call I got about my wardrobe.

That's why when I got invited to the White House Correspondents' Dinner again a year later, in spring 2018, I wore a bold color. Big hair. Big jewelry. And I walked in with renowned Spanish chef José Andrés and his wife as my dates, while my husband cheered me on from home. (I only got one ticket.) I felt beautiful and proud to look *very* Latina.

I never did personally confront that higher-up at work about the phone call. But the next time something about my appearance came up, I was prepared to defend myself.

It happened about four months later at the office, when this person raised an objection about my red lipstick. I went back to my desk around the corner for a couple of minutes, took a deep breath, confided in my best friend at the network, and went back out to the larger newsroom.

"If what you have to say doesn't directly impact my editorial or the story I'm covering, I would appreciate it if you refrained from those kinds of comments in the future," I said.

This person was sitting at their computer, and other folks in the office probably heard. We didn't talk about it anymore. It never happened again.

I'm done pretending that it is okay to be treated as if I'm from a different planet. I will fight against it not only for me but for Alondra de la Cruz, the student I mentor who texted to tell me she got accepted to UC Berkley to study journalism. And Alberto Solórzano, the principal at Marilyn Elementary in California who asked me to read to his class in Spanish and English because his students were terrified after recent immigration raids. Or the kids at Nora Sandigo's home in Miami, whose story I told on NBC *Nightly News*—she takes in children whose parents get deported or who fear deportation. By becoming their legal guardian, she saves them from entering the overcrowded foster care and immigration systems. She has received signed power of attorney documents for more than 1,250 minors. It's a great responsibility that she takes on every day with the help of many volunteers.

For all of them. For my husband. For our future kids. For all the "different" ones. For you. I am going to be unapologetically myself—unapologetically Latina.

#GoLikeMariana: We can't choose what we look like or where we come from. But we do get to choose how we use the power that each one of us has, big or small, to help worthy causes. Let's celebrate our differences and make them building blocks, not rocks to throw at each other.

4

A Human Bridge

New York City, 2001

It was 8:55 a.m., September 11, 2001.

"Papi, *por qué*? Why can't I sleep in on the last day of my summer vacation?" I mumbled as my father hastily woke me up sometime before my alarm clock.

My Tweety Bird slippers and seventeen-year-old attitude sluggishly made their way to the kitchen.

I saw my dad standing there, motionless, staring at the images projected on the TV. I looked at the screen. I didn't understand what was happening.

A building—which I recognized as one of the Twin Towers—was in flames.

We were standing about six miles north of the World Trade Center.

At 9:03 a.m. another aircraft crashed into the second tower, like a jolt confirming our worst fears. My sister, Graciela, and I watched, still doubting our eyes. It was like an action movie turned horror film.

My father trembled as he held our plane tickets in his hand. We were scheduled to fly back to Venezuela from JFK that day at 5:00 p.m.

I had flown to NYC to meet up with my family for summer vacation. My mom and younger brother had returned home a day before because his school started earlier. Also, my parents always insisted on not flying together on the same aircraft. "What if something happened to the two of us at the same time? Who would take care of the kids?" they reasoned.

So Papi, Graciela, and I had stayed an extra day, just long enough to witness the devastation of the city we had come to think of as our second home.

My dad loved New York. When Venezuela's economy was thriving after the oil boom in the seventies, he saved up enough money to buy a small place in the city. He told us he felt like the "King of the World," calling New York his new neighborhood.

Over time Dad sold his beloved apartment and got another one, on the Upper East Side. That's where we stayed at the end of summer, year after year, before returning to Venezuela, and where my family stays when we're in town. Those vacations helped us grow up in a world of contrasts, with two cities we could easily call home for different reasons.

Over the years I have watched New York and our neighborhood there change dramatically. When I was a child, inexpensive clothing stores and a burger shack were in the basement of our place; now there are stores that sell designer watches and exclusive jewelry. Mami often complains about having to walk several blocks to buy a decent-priced carton of milk and catch the subway. The gaps have become bigger due to gentrification.

Still, NYC is a metropolis where I can anonymously slip into the crowd and be in the thick of it. No labels. No constraints. I sit in the subway. I run in the park. I go to museums and churches. It's a relationship to a city I never had with Caracas. That morning in 2001, however, that sense of safety was deeply shaken.

My sister and I held hands for more than an hour as we watched the desperate attempts to get people out of the towers: security personnel trying to clear the buildings, fires burning through both structures, people throwing themselves from the windows in an attempt to survive or die quickly.

We were tuned in to the *TODAY Show* on NBC, where journalists such as Katie Couric, Al Roker, and many others walked us through what was happening, helping us grapple with the indescribable. I learned the value of context and nuance that day. The importance of finding out why the terrorists wanted to destroy America and how they were able to plan the attacks.

The sudden burst of our security bubble wiped out my view of the world, changing the country and changing everything for us immigrants.

It would take me much longer to understand the full implications of the most horrendous terrorist attack in the history of the United States, but my father knew right away. I had never seen my hero look so helpless. He just stood there, somewhere between numb and shocked.

The next hours were marked by frantic attempts to locate our friends in the city and call the airlines. My godfather, Leopoldo Monterrey; his wife, Maria Isabel; and their seven-year-old child, Juan, had gone to the airport to catch an early flight back to Venezuela, but we could not contact them.

Leo was a tall, athletic writer, my dad's free-spirited best friend. I had just picked him that year as the adult who would guide me in my faith during my confirmation, a position that Catholics honor. A *padrino* becomes a second father.

I felt that if some day, God forbid, something were to happen to my parents, he would be the best person to take care of us. However, having him in the city that day was a realization that I could lose both my dad and my godfather in one sweep.

Every minute of not knowing whether he and his family were alive was agonizing. It's a feeling I have come to know very well as a journalist on the field, when I see people searching for family or friends amid disaster.

On September 11, we weren't worried just about the Monterreys. We were also praying for so many good people in the city whom we had come to know over the years, from Spencer, the owner of

Throckmorton Fine Art—a gallery my dad loved to visit—to the local fruit vendor who wasn't at his post that morning.

Are they all okay? How long will we have to stay in New York City? The airspace is shut down. What will happen to us?

"Papi, we have no food!" I yelled from the kitchen.

"A Venezuelan died in the attacks," he said with the phone in his hand. "There are victims from all over the world." I was overcome by a sense of shared mortality that went beyond borders and nationalities.

As it turned out, Leo and his family were rescheduled to travel back home on an earlier flight. But we did not know this yet. When the attack happened, the Monterreys were checking in at the airport counter in JFK and an airline employee whispered something into the ear of the woman who was helping them. The woman's face turned pale.

"It's not one of ours," the airline employee said.

A state of alert swept around the airport, but not a state of emergency—yet.

Leo had been waiting at the gate with his family for an hour or so when he heard a dreadful announcement: "We are evacuating the airport. You have to leave—now!"

They still had no sense of how bad the situation was. He said his wife didn't want to leave without her suitcase. When they reached the baggage area, everyone was rushing out.

"When we finally got our bags and dragged them outside, nobody was there. We were one of the last people to exit JFK airport on 9/11," Leo later told me.

There were no cabs. They started walking with their bags. His seven-year-old carried his own little suitcase.

They eventually spotted a man driving an empty bus, and they stopped him. "*Señor,* please take us wherever you are going."

The bus took them to Queens. As they got out, bags in hand, they witnessed the throngs desperately trying to leave the nightmare behind.

Some crossed bridges on foot. Others ran away from Manhattan like a stampede of ghosts, most of their faces covered with dust.

Meanwhile, in our apartment we were going crazy. We didn't know if Leo and his family had actually made it to the airport or not.

While my dad worked the phones, I had to go get some provisions.

I ran out in my pajamas and sneakers, trying to find a supermarket. There was no time to change, no time to think. Nothing could prepare me for what I was about to witness.

I breathed in as I saw a cloud of smoke devouring buildings and structures. I was farther uptown, but I could still see it. I don't remember how far down I went.

I started panting; I was about to experience my first anxiety attack.

People around me were running, crying tears of frustration. Some were holding handkerchiefs over their mouths. I will never forget the despair in their eyes.

I was able to get some cereal boxes and milk before rushing back to the apartment.

In Queens, Leo spotted a driving school called Ferrari. The sign on the door read "We Are Closed," but he knocked on the window anyway, hoping to provide his family with a place to stay safe. The owners—Latinos—came to the door.

"*Sí, entren.*" They opened the door and took in Leo, Maria Isabel, and Juan for about two hours.

Finally, Leo noticed people heading to the subway, which had reopened by then. There was practically no one trying to get back to Manhattan, but Leo wanted to get to us. They took the subway all the way to 59th Street. When they got out, for the first time they witnessed New York City as a silent town.

They walked and walked until a cab driver gave them a lift to our neighborhood.

I couldn't believe it when I saw them in our building lobby. They looked stunned, grateful to be alive, as if they had come back from another world.

I ran toward them.

"*Ahijada querida*," Leo said, opening his arms wide. "My dearest goddaughter." We hugged each other for the longest time.

Even though they were the ones who had been lost in the nightmare, I, too, felt as if I had been lost—and found.

As the sun set on the day of the attack, many of our neighbors slowly started coming down to the street level, outside their front lobbies, to light candles and talk. It was an extended vigil that acted as a gathering so people wouldn't feel alone. Still, we were all scared.

We had to stay in the city until they resumed international flights. We didn't know how long it would take. Logistically we had a small problem: none of us could cook! Most of the restaurants and takeout services weren't working, so we mostly ate cereal.

For a week or two, nobody could go to work. A city that's always on the go had been brought to a shrieking halt.

One night we went down to 57th Street and encountered a scene so serene that it was strikingly beautiful. Hundreds of candles filled the usually bustling intersection. In the wake of insurmountable pain, strangers and neighbors chose to comfort each other, to band together with a sense of ownership toward the city.

New Yorkers left their homes to pray, to share food, to connect, and to grieve collectively.

A week after 9/11 we still didn't know what to do. Staying indoors and watching the news was unbearable. But we were afraid of stepping out. Could we go to the movies? What about the Metropolitan Museum? What if there was a bomb around the Empire State Building? There was uncertainty and waiting. Everyone feared another attack.

Papi knew things were going to change drastically. It had been a traumatic experience for the whole world. There would be an international crisis. War. More pain and destruction.

I remember we walked around Central Park a great deal. It was the only spot that felt somewhat safe. We didn't dare go near Ground Zero.

One day we went up Madison Avenue, where we spotted the first person we'd seen eating at a restaurant. He was wearing a New York Yankees hat and a dark-brown suede coat and was sitting outside. Alone. Defiant. I didn't know his name or his story, but I knew what he was saying to everyone who walked past him: "We can't let them take our way of life." He didn't need to speak; the message of his presence was loud and clear.

My dad turned to me and said, "Mari, I want you to look at that man and learn this lesson: Resilience. The human capacity to adapt and overcome adversity. And," he added, "doing it gracefully."

The political ramifications of September 11 came months later, during President Bush's State of the Union Address in January 2002: "Iraq, North Korea, Iran . . . states like these and their terrorist allies, constitute an axis of evil," President Bush said. "These regimes pose a grave and growing danger."

Being from Venezuela—at the time governed by President Hugo Chávez, an outspoken critic of the US who had declared himself an ally of Iran—I knew exactly which side my country was on. I was split between two places, grappling with two opposing ideologies.

So from that moment on, I made a conscious effort to reconcile those opposite narratives with my own. I wanted to move seamlessly between my worlds to evaluate the best and worst in each one. To be a human bridge—to show that people on one side were just like the ones on the other. I kept thinking about Maya Angelou's famous quote: "We are more alike, my friends, than we are unalike." Why is it so hard for some to understand that we are basically all one and the same?

I saw this truth in small, hopeful moments that began to show themselves in the city following the attacks. One of my fondest memories of healing was the 2002 NYC Marathon. In 2001, it was canceled over safety concerns, just two months after the attacks, but the city invited runners to sign up for the following year.

Attendance in 2002 was massive. Leo ran it as I cheered him on, and I promised myself I would participate at least once in my life as a show of my love to New York City. (I finally ran it in 2010!) The runners in the streets made their comebacks, the ultimate show of resilience.

Ten years later, in 2011, I was in New York during the takedown of Osama Bin Laden by US Special Forces. I went down to the World Trade Center with my own little camera and filmed the tears and hugs of so many people who would finally have some measure of closure that day.

Every time I returned to the US, however, there was just a little more looking over the shoulder and a little more isolation. A little more fear. Many got the sense that America, once a beacon of hope, had started on a path toward unexamined nationalism and fearmongering. Remembering those clouds of smoke, the smell, and the fear in people's eyes, I understood it. We had a reason to be afraid. We'd seen what unchecked hatred of "the others" (the West) could cause. But that's the thing about fear; no one tells you it's natural to be afraid—that you don't have to generalize, categorize, and demonize in order to explain it away. This fear of the other, on both sides, creates a gulf between people—one that needs to be bridged if we are ever going to live in peace. Witnessing this fear would change my way of seeing the world.

After all, I was not from around these parts; I was from the real south—South America. From a part of the world that often gets negative media coverage and is referred to in the news as "third world"; its people are called "illegal aliens" or "the others." This girl from Caracas could be the bridge between worlds, between languages, between ages and generations, to help people see the struggles but also the beauty that each culture, each human being has to offer.

I couldn't fight terror with political or military might, but I could do it with stories. The ones that connect us—that shine a light in the darkness of our fears.

#*Go like Mariana*: In the face of terror, our greatest strengths are resilience—the human capacity to adapt and overcome adversity—and remembering that we are more alike than unalike.

5

Freedom Is Never Free

Caracas, 2007

Tear gas smells the same everywhere: Caracas, Ferguson, or Hong Kong. It doesn't matter where you are. It's unmistakable, and it reeks of repression.

When you see it has dispersed in the air, you think you have escaped and that you're okay. But thirty seconds after exposure, the effects kick in. You get a burning, watery sensation in the eyes and experience shortness of breath, uncontrollable drooling, and skin irritation. It later morphs into a choking sensation, as if someone started crushing your chest, making it impossible to move. Finally, vomiting and diarrhea ensure you don't forget the experience for the rest of the day—or, in my case, the rest of my life.

Tear gas is considered a chemical warfare agent under the Geneva Convention. Its use has been prohibited in war since 1993. But in 2007, I would endure its devastating impact for the first time.

I was a twenty-three-year-old college junior, majoring in mass communications at the Universidad Católica Andrés Bello in Caracas—a university that publicly opposed the Chávez government, accusing them of violating human rights. And we were not going to take it silently.

For me, the heat of those summer months is saturated in my memory with fear—the smell of tear gas, the charged energy of student protests, and the gut-wrenching terror I would experience a few months later on the hike that changed the course of my life. With a gun to my head, I would face death when I still hadn't had the courage to really do what I wanted with my life, to pursue my calling. In the swirling chaos of it all, I would struggle to make sense of my way forward and to break free of the repression that clouded the very air we breathed.

When I had signed up for my undergraduate program in 2003 at La Católica, I had three concentration choices: advertising, film-making, or journalism. In my heart—especially after living through 9/11—I wanted to choose the latter. Yet by the time I had to declare a major, three years in, attacks on journalists in my home country were sky-high. They faced violence and harassment from government forces who sought to control the narrative at any cost. I feared for my future and, amid my frustration, opted to play it safe by choosing advertising.

Qué miedosa. What a cowardly move, Mariana.

My parents were at ease with the idea that I wasn't going to expose myself to the dangers and criticisms of being a reporter—as long as I was happy. My first part-time job while in college was at advertising giant BBDO in Venezuela. I was training to eventually be an account manager. But I was miserable. Within a few months I knew that was not what I wanted to do with my life.

Our region of South America was going through turbulent times, and I couldn't peel myself away. I wanted to have a front-row seat to history and be a part of the generation that took action.

After five years in power, the Chávez government was beginning to show its authoritarian colors and desire to hold on to power. Students started rising up. We were inspired by our history books and what we had read about Mahatma Gandhi, Martin Luther King Jr., and a group of Venezuelan students back in the day called the Generation of 1928 who rose up against the dictatorship of Juan Vicente Gómez. That uprising had been the first successful mass movement in our country, which laid the groundwork for our democracy and set the path for leaders who would become presidents of the republic in the twentieth century.

When I walked the halls of La Católica, the announcement from President Hugo Chávez that he was shutting down Radio Caracas Television (RCTV) hit us like a ton of bricks, especially in the communication school.

Many of my classmates were already experienced student leaders and protesters who had mobilized to demand justice for students affected by violence and bad policy. I wasn't a leader or organizer by any means, nor were my siblings, who went to the same college. But we knew it was our time to rise up with the rest of the student body. It was a process of gradual empowerment. Gradually we realized—individually and collectively—that we had the ability to affect the reality that surrounded us. We were indignant. We clamored for change.

By 2007, we had planted the seeds: a sense of responsibility and a strong, organized support system from the whole student body and the other eight colleges in Caracas.

Every day there was a new student assembly where the leaders told the movement about the protest activity for the day, whether it was marching, debating, participating in a sit-in or a town hall, or raising money. Our teachers cheered us on.

The movement didn't have a hierarchical structure. Different groups just started assuming different roles. There were the spokespeople, groups that made banners, groups that coordinated traffic, groups that rallied the crowds, and groups that ran social media.

The whole class came out of its cocoon with powerful wings.

With the RCTV shutdown, Chávez managed to cut off people who didn't have any other windows to the outside world or any other outlets to denounce the wrongs in their neighborhoods. He suppressed the poorest slums, those he had pledged to defend. In 2002, the station gave airtime to the leaders of a failed coup d'état against his government. He vowed to make them pay.

It was the same old dictatorial script he learned in Fidel Castro's

Cuba: silencing the press to control information, both inside the country and internationally.

That act of injustice sparked something powerful in me. It was the lightning rod that made me own up to the fact that I wanted to be the journalist who brought to light what those in power were fiercely trying to cover.

We would not back down. Freedom of speech and of the press was our raison d'être. My classmates and I kept staging forums, sit-ins, and rallies. We were getting a crash course in democracy.

Five days after the network's shutdown, we planned a peaceful demonstration: a march from our university, in the outskirts of Caracas, to the Catholic Church's Episcopal Conference building. We wanted the church to help us mediate a conversation with the government. We needed an advocate that would give our cause gravitas and give us guidance and protection.

The whole student body, approximately three thousand people, planned to participate in the mile-and-a-half walk. Our biggest challenge lay on the other side of the school gate.

The gate was a simple metal door made of thin wire, and it was where we hung out during breaks or where I sometimes secretly shared a cigarette with my friends between classes. (I was never a smoker, but every once in a while I would take a drag or two, trying to be "cool.") But that spring, the weak school gate had acquired an entirely different meaning. It had become a defensive wall, the only thing separating us from hundreds of National Guard troops outfitted similarly to riot police—decked in black commando gear, holding long guns, Plexiglas shields, and tear gas bombs, and willing to do everything to stop us from marching.

We painted our hands white as a sign of peace. We carried banners that read "Freedom" and "We are just students." Some girls even held carnations, which they gave to the troops as a symbol of solidarity, attempting to soften their hearts.

Nice try.

"The students will *not* pass!" the colonel in charge screamed through his loudspeaker. "If you don't go back to class, we will be forced to repel this march!"

We responded in unison: "*¿Quiénes somos?*—Who are we? *¡Estudiantes!*—Students!" We clapped and clamored.

"What do we want? *Freedom!*"

Libertad.

As time passed, confrontation became unavoidable. I was standing alongside Graciela, who was an undergraduate law student in my same year, and Alvaro Elias, four years younger than me, just starting college, but already a man.

For the three of us, being a part of the movement was organic. We had passionate conversations at the dinner table about our role as the next generation. About the fact that if you were a student, you had a responsibility to stand up for free speech, freedom of the press, and democracy. Our parents supported us, even marching with us in our neighborhood's streets on weekends. There was a power vacuum; their own generation had failed us. They were scared for us, but also *orgullosos*, proud to see us lead. Still, Mami would say, "Don't go to the front of the march. Don't do anything stupid!"

Back at the protest, her words echoed in my head as I realized my brother had brought handkerchiefs for us to cover our faces with. A small towel with milk or vinegar is a homemade remedy against the effects of tear gas. When I noticed he had his kit ready, I knew he had every intention of heading to the front of the protest. My sister wanted to stay toward the back.

My priority was to protect them and document whatever happened with my camera. (This was before the days of iPhones and streaming.) My family, my civil rights, my future—absolutely everything was at risk.

The guards had helmets with transparent shields. We could make eye contact. They stared blankly; they only knew how to obey orders. We could see the look of hate that Chávez's movement had sown so deep that it pitted us against one another.

Quick inhale.

Time ran out.

The gate opened.

The carnations fell to the ground.

I felt a hint of sweat on my sister's hand as she held on tight. My brother tightened the handkerchief around his head and moved away from us.

"Students!" we screamed with our white-painted hands in the air as we ran toward the National Guard like Vikings.

The army fired pellets at us. They fired bullets at the sky. They opened the water cannons so the cold jets would slam us.

But the worst was the gas.

The range of a tear gas bomb can be between six hundred and four thousand square feet. The cloud of poisonous smoke covered us like in a *Star Wars* battle scene. I was holding on to my sister, but I couldn't see her anymore. The smell, the ardor, the fear— everything was mixed in this dark haze.

The angst of losing her hit me harder than the gases, the shoving, and the stomping. I wanted to scream her name. My voice faltered.

Where was my sister? How would I find her? I couldn't see my younger brother either.

Hours later I found Graciela and Alvaro Elias on the other side of the gate. That separation, in that last march we attended together, was an omen of how our paths would soon diverge. Our home was crumbling around us.

After the march, protests continued undaunted. Every morning we went to class with our backpacks filled with banners, markers, and battle plans.

"So, kids, where are you going to march this *mañana*?" Professor Jerry O'Sullivan would ask with a Gaelic accent as we strolled into his communications class with dark circles under our eyes.

Mr. O'Sullivan was an Irishman from the town of Rathbarry. He was in his seventies, with short white hair, and he was always decked out in a bow tie and jacket (in that Caribbean heat!). I never knew why or how he ended up teaching our class, but I was grateful to have our own real-life Lucky Charms character. Later I found out that this humble grandpa-type was a Stanford scholar and a former Legionary (or soldier of the church) and had received a knighthood in the Order of St. Gregory—the highest honor the Catholic Church can give a layperson.

We had formed a special bond, and he had become genuinely interested in my future. He said I should consider going to the

United States, because with my English and good grades I could surely qualify for a merit scholarship.

"You have a lot of *potencial*," Jerry would say. "You can't let your circumstances define you," he went on. "Sometimes the best way to help is from afar."

But in my heart, I didn't want to leave. I was enamored with what we were doing at the student movement; this was what I wanted to be a part of.

For that entire year I marched during the day, went to my part-time job at the ad agency, and watched the American news at night. Our parents had installed a small satellite dish at home so we could keep up with learning the English language. They brought us books, DVDs, and any other material in English they could find.

My favorite news shows were *60 Minutes*, *World News*, and the *TODAY Show*. I admired the gravitas of Andrea Mitchell, with her knowledge of foreign politics; the voice, style, and depth of Diane Sawyer, who looked like a movie star; and the friendliness and sparkle of Katie Couric.

I was finally certain of what I wanted to do in life. I dreamed of being Mariana, the journalist. I wanted to be on TV. But I kept my secret to myself, because I knew it was a dangerous job in my corner of the world, and I wasn't clear about how far I was willing to go to get a story.

As the gaps grew between the Chávez administration and the opposition, and the hatred grew between both sides, reporters started getting arrested and were forced to flee for not cooperating with the government. Others got shamed for being too extreme in criticizing the president. I understood it would have been impossible to do the kind of journalism I do today from Venezuela.

I had been juggling the student protest and my secret longing to be a journalist on the Sunday morning when I went on the hike that made my entire life flash before my eyes. There I was on my knees, panting, with the muzzle of a gun to my head. The words of 2 Timothy 1:7 from my King James Bible came rushing to my head amid the terror: "For God hath not given us the spirit of fear; but of power, and of love, and of a sound mind."

Power. Love. A sound mind. They are the answers to terror. And the keys to finding purpose. The mugging signaled a before and an after. I had to pursue my calling. If I made it off that mountain, everything would change.

The night of the mugging, my body still trembling from fright, I showered twice but couldn't wash away the encounter. I decided to confide in my closest ally.

My slippers made their way slowly toward Papi's study, a room filled with books, art objects, and its characteristic walls painted forest green; a room we lovingly called the green room. That's where Dad spent his nights reading and listening to classical music. As I got closer, I heard the melody of the song "As Time Goes By" from the movie *Casablanca*, our favorite.

I took it as a good sign.

"Papi, I need to talk to you," I said.

"Of course, *mi* Mari. What do you have in mind?" he answered as he closed his book, put down his little tequila glass, and looked up at me.

"I was thinking about my future, and . . . umm . . . I—I've decided I want to be a journalist. A TV journalist."

He smiled.

"*Mi* Mari, I raised you to be whatever you want in life. I have given you and will continue to give you everything I can to develop that passion within you. If you want to be a journalist, I'll support you unconditionally.

"But remember, nothing is ever free. You have to work hard to achieve what you want."

He raised his glass ceremoniously and said, "Cheers to my daughter, Mariana, the journalist."

That was the blessing I needed. But I could have saved myself a lot of time had I just spoken up earlier.

Often, especially when we are young, we're embarrassed to say what we envision for ourselves—we're mortified to be open about who and what we love and to truly articulate what we want for our lives—because it might not fit into what our families or society dictates. But if we keep our dreams secret, no one will come ask us about them. Once we've deciphered what we want for ourselves, an important next step is to tell the world about it. The more we say it out loud, the more real it'll become. And guess what? People around will actually be inclined to help. So shout your dreams from the rooftops!

Having confessed my dreams out into the world, I now needed to put in the work. I had to move quickly. I needed to complete the GMAT or the GRE, get recommendation letters, and start the application process for a list of schools whose programs interested me.

I channeled the trauma into to-do lists. That same week I bought colored binders, Sharpie pens, and a big calendar for application deadlines.

Then I set out to look for a journalistic image and style I wanted to emulate. My first sources of inspiration were Katie, Diane, and Andrea—ladies with caring and strong personalities. But they all looked so different from the young girl who dreamed of being like them, sitting on the other side of her TV screen in South America. I certainly didn't have their English intonation, golden hair, or delicate features.

Searching for role models, I discovered Christiane Amanpour. Ever since I saw her for the first time I'd recorded all her stories onto VHS tapes with a sticker that read "Do not delete" in black magic marker.

Amanpour. What a woman, with her black rebellious mane, Iranian-British accent, olive-colored skin, and safari outfits. She could speak different languages, chase Osama Bin Laden through the mountains, and cover wars as well as any of her male colleagues. If only I could be as fearless as she was.

As I dealt with the application process, I was also dealing with a lot of self-defeating fear. About my test scores. About the competition.

Professor O'Sullivan gave me the encouragement I needed for my applications.

"You have *muy buenos* grades and a life story that makes you *diferente*," he said.

He encouraged me to stop reading generic college application advice online and focus on writing an essay from my heart. His advice was on point: whether you're applying to school or the job of your dreams, own what makes you special. Cookie cutter won't get anyone past the pile of essays or job applications.

I stopped listening to my head, and *le hice caso a O'Sullivan.* I listened to my professor.

My college application essay ended up being an open letter to President Chávez, pleading with him to put an end to the division and hatred in our land. It conveyed my plea and commitment as a future journalist. To end my letter, I concluded:

> While as humans we will never be entirely objective, journalists must fight against imbalanced coverage, regardless of an organization's or government's tendencies. Thanks to you, Mr. President, I learned this lesson the hard way. . . . I know you'll hate me for this, sir, but I will soon start as intern at Globovisión, the only remaining station that disparages your administration. However, cognizant of the channel's partiality, I know the only way I'll become a balanced reporter is to pursue a graduate journalism program. . . .
>
> After graduate school, maybe I'll see you again. Maybe you'll see me. I'll be the one behind the anchor's chair or correspondent's desk at an international news organization. From there, I'll change the perspective on journalism in Venezuela

and be a leader in the news business. Ultimately, my aim is to participate thoughtfully in the way people perceive reality, because the world isn't red [the color most often associated with communism], Mr. President, much less black or white.

In truth you've helped, sir, as the events I've experienced firsthand have provided me with a keen eye that sees more than good or evil. The distorted view of journalism in my country has instilled in me a desire for change that can only be a trait of the most persistent.

Thank you for everything.

Sincerely, Mariana Atencio

October 2007

My letter broke through. The university deans took notice. Over the phone, some told me that letter stood out from most of the application packets they read.

While I'd applied to four schools, I had my heart set on Columbia, because New York City was my second home. I still remember the feeling of excitement that took hold of my body when I read an email revealing the chance of a lifetime.

Dear Ms. Atencio: We are pleased to inform you, you have been awarded a full-merit scholarship to attend Columbia University's School of Journalism . . .

It was the springboard to freedom and safety in one sentence— one that had God's touch written all over it.

But my achievement was bittersweet. The tear gas bombs kept spreading all over the skies of my city. My classmates continued to risk their lives every day. I was overcome by guilt, as if I were betraying them. I felt as if I were about to win a relay race and then stopped abruptly, one second before crossing the finish line.

My mom stepped in. She was more practical and direct in her approach. I came upon her reading in her chaise longue, every bit the lady of our house, with her easy elegance and beauty.

Her warm smile shone on me as she put the book down while gesturing for me to sit next to her. I hugged her, letting her delicate fragrance and soft kisses on my head cover me. Her embrace is the best way to describe what home feels like.

Her words were firm, but gentle and full of emotion. That's her style.

"Mari, we love you more than you will ever know. It will be extremely hard for us to see you leave, but we know that's the only way for you to find your own path. You can't stay here! We will never forgive ourselves if you lost this opportunity because you feel as if you need to stay to take care of us.

"The bond we share is unbreakable. No matter how far you or your siblings travel or for how long, we are one, like a hand with its five fingers. Each one is equally important. We can spread them open or put them close together. Handshake to greet friends or raised fist against injustice. That's us."

This time it was Mami—Lady Diana, as some of my friends call her—who gave me the push I needed. I got on that plane and promised not to look back. If I was going, I would have to move forward.

#Go like Mariana: If we keep our dreams secret, no one will come ask us about them. Once we've deciphered what we want for ourselves, an important next step is to tell the world about it. The more we say it out loud, the more real it'll become.

6

Mariana the Journalist

New York City, 2009

I could barely contain my excitement. The great Christiane Amanpour was going to be at our campus at Columbia University.

Amanpour and her famed CNN colleague Anderson Cooper were both scheduled to give speeches at the journalism school. Most of my classmates lined up to take pictures with "the silver fox," but I wanted a photo with my hero.

After her lecture, I noticed she dashed out quickly through one of the hallways. *I bet she's going after Bin Laden*, I thought.

I ran across the auditorium to talk to her before she reached the elevator, where my classmate was standing, starstruck.

"I admire you so much," I told her as I snapped a quick photo of her next to my friend. "I'm sorry, I know you're in a hurry. Where are you headed?"

"I have to take my son to the dentist," she replied with a half smile.

Definitely not the answer I was anticipating. But it was a real moment between two women at different points in their careers—one that made me realize women will always need to wear different hats, have different roles, and be expected to execute all of them well. Amanpour, a veteran journalist, a warrior, had to be a mother first when her child needed her.

My biggest challenges to this day are being a working woman in news who wishes to have more family time and being an immigrant who wants to give a voice to those who need it most. I've learned to discover the incredible strengths behind both identities instead of considering them a burden. With every different hat and different role—unexpected or otherwise—comes a new strength.

After the turmoil in Venezuela, I arrived in the United States on August 5, 2008—without a return ticket. I had a Spanish accent, no green card, and a suitcase filled with dreams that seemed impossible at the time. But I knew this was what Papi meant when he said,

"You never know what the future holds." This is what he had been preparing me for. Migrating is what the future held for me.

During my year of graduate school, I started telling stories in English for the first time. It was a pivotal moment in America, and as a journalism student, I got to cover it all. The historic election of President Barack Obama, the first black president in the nation's history, stood out among the assignments.

When the election results were announced, I was covering the story for school at the headquarters of the Obama campaign in Philadelphia, a city rich with African American history.

I went out to the streets and saw dozens of people of all races and creeds hugging and even dancing joyfully. I thought about all the hatred and division I had witnessed in my own country, and I felt relieved by what I was seeing in this city. It looked like the beginning of an era of equality and acceptance.

Having arrived to "post-racial America" made me feel so lucky. (Boy, little did I know what was coming!)

After an eventful year of study, I proudly walked through Columbia's spectacular campus on 116th and Broadway to the sound of "New York, New York" by Frank Sinatra in my light blue cap and gown.

I was surrounded by some pretty amazing classmates and future colleagues. Many had a ton of professional experience. During my year at Columbia, I had periodically suffered from the inescapable imposter syndrome. I tortured myself thinking, *What can I possibly contribute here? Maybe they made a mistake with my scholarship. Everyone is way more qualified than I am. They already have job offers.*

But that day with my cap and gown, listening to ol' blue eyes, I felt truly ready to take on the world.

My biggest motivation: my parents' faces. They managed to go to the ceremony and were simply beaming with pride. *Orgullosos*.

Unlike most of my classmates, I needed a visa to work legally in the United States when I graduated from Columbia. No English-speaking network was hiring anyone who didn't have at least a green card. Plus, any company that hired me would need to pay extra for my sponsorship. This was a huge handicap, especially in the middle of a recession. It was like going to a job interview with a sticky note on your forehead that read "Don't hire me."

After having the door shut in my face many times, I decided to use my apparent disadvantages, what made me different, as competitive advantages: my immigrant status, my Spanish, and my knowledge of Latin America. Transforming perceived flaws into positive tools can make us stand out and be successful wherever we find ourselves.

That's how I managed to get my foot in the door, albeit the back door, at the newspaper *El Diario*, the oldest Spanish newspaper in the United States.

Most of us won't get to the top by riding the elevator; we will have to take the stairs. But we will relish that staircase—the journey.

I was very proud to have landed a job in journalism, even as an intern, in the middle of the Great Recession. Almost nine million people lost their jobs in the United States between 2008 and 2009. Of these, 114,000 newsroom employees, reporters, editors, photographers, and videographers—working in five industries that produce news: newspaper, radio, broadcast television, cable, and digital news publishing—lost their jobs, according to the Pew Research Center.

I didn't really have any negotiating room. I had no green card. But my boss had approved sponsoring my work visa. While it wasn't my dream job in broadcasting, I recognized that it was an absolutely critical step along the way. And I couldn't afford to lose it.

By now I think we know each other well enough for me to confess that my biggest letdowns come when I appear to be riding the crest of the wave. That happened in my first job in journalism. I had been working at *El Diario* for almost a year, and I thought I was on the fast track up the success ladder. And when I least expected it, I fell—hard.

My day started out on cloud nine because I'd gotten an interview with the famous Chilean author Isabel Allende. It wasn't a minor feat. Isabel, who had penned the book *The House of the Spirits* and was considered the most widely read Spanish author in the world, had just published a new novel, *Island Beneath the Sea*, and I was going to interview her.

I hopped on to the subway from Spanish Harlem to Brooklyn with a skip in my step, savoring the way I would write the interview, emphasizing the beauty of Latin American magical realism and female empowerment, two common themes in Isabel's work.

Upon reaching the outside lobby of the building where the paper's offices were, I ran into my best friend, Ana Maria, who was just zipping in with her scooter. She was wearing Converse sneakers and a red T-shirt that read "Seriously?" in bold white letters, its capped sleeve revealing a henna tattoo.

Ana wanted to code digital content, and since *El Diario* needed an intern, I had handed in her résumé to help her out. After all, I had started out as an intern too, and they hired me a few months later.

I was twenty-five and Ana was twenty-three, but she looked fifteen. She was my Peter Pan. I am sure Ana came up with the mantra YOLO before it became trendy. And no matter how many years go by, she always looks like a teenager, with the spirit of a restless rebel.

"*¡Hola, chama!* Hey, girl!" We gave each other a kiss on the cheek as is customary in Latin America, and I handed her some light pudding snacks I had bought for us that morning.

"This is to watch *la dieta*, our diet. *Por favor*, don't look at me like that. Being single we gotta stay in shape," I told her with a motherly smile.

"Don't be a pain in my butt, Mariana! I want pudding with *all* the calories. Why do I want to have some size-two wedding photos? *¿Pa' qué?* So that if I jump to double digits later I'll have my husband nagging me because he didn't marry someone who was a size ten? No, no, no," she replied, rolling her eyes as she took the bag and whisked her scooter to the elevator door.

When the doors opened on the eighteenth floor, I realized something was wrong.

The newsroom at *El Diario* was typically a colorful environment where you would see all sorts of characters wandering about, like Hispanic congresswoman Nydia Velásquez, the astrologer known as the Child Prodigy (*El Niño Prodigio*), and Peruvian journalist Vicky Peláez, later accused of spying on behalf of Russia. But today it looked like a funeral scene.

At the door we ran into people we had never seen before. All very serious, dressed in black, they looked like a sort of diplomatic delegation from the underworld. We noticed everyone lowered their voices. They mumbled in scattered groups in the corners. You could cut the tension with a knife.

"What's happening?" Ana asked, concerned.

"I'll find out. You go to the library. Don't worry," I replied.

I didn't have an office—not even a cubicle or a desk. Ana and I shared a space in a small, windowless room dubbed the library, which was filled with old books, piles of newspapers, and dust. We had the worst allergies at the end of every workweek.

I was far away from working at a TV network. But in that hole-in-the-wall filled with dust, I officially became a journalist. It was there where I first wrote articles about the Hispanic community in New York. Some were about serious topics, and others, well, were on the lighter side, like the pieces I wrote about the firefighters' calendar, the city's parades with its dazzling floats, and even a porn convention. Obviously, this wasn't the TV job I'd aspired to get when I graduated from Columbia. But it was mine, and I needed it for more reasons than one.

That somber morning I scanned the place looking for my boss in the sea of people in black suits. He was coming toward me. His face was red. His Argentinian blue eyes looked as if they were about to burst into tears.

"Atencio, today of all days, *no revientes mi paciencia*—don't try my temper!" he snapped as he walked down the hallway with the black crows.

I had never witnessed someone getting laid off. But I was very aware of the tough state of the economy and how it affected the whole country, and the world.

Even so, I never thought they would fire me.

"Miss Mariana Atencio? Come with us please," one of the men in black said.

Breathe, Mariana—respira.

They guided me to a glass office where they were taking away some of the furniture and the personal objects of its previous occupant.

"We regret to inform you that we are letting you go. Your position is no longer available."

That was all. I stopped breathing for about five seconds. It was the most robotic exchange I had experienced in my entire life.

I realized the black crow who guided me here was part of a company in charge of firing people. It reminded me of the 2009 movie *Up in the Air,* but unfortunately the guy who delivered my bad news looked nothing like George Clooney.

I was distraught. *What now?*

Quickly the image of Mariana the journalist faded. It was gone as fast as the flowerpot they were packing up.

"What about my visa?" was the only thing I uttered through the knot in my throat. "You see, the newspaper already sponsored it. And if I lose it I won't be able to legally stay in the United States," I argued, thinking *that* would surely convince them to help me.

"Miss Atencio, we are letting go of one-third of this company. Right now your visa is not one of our concerns."

They handed me a yellow piece of paper: a list of everyone who was being let go that day, including their first name, last name, age, and duration in the company.

"Pack up your things, and leave the building as soon as possible please."

I was just a number in their corporate America. There were people on the list who were more than sixty years old and who probably had mortgages, kids in college, and families to feed, but none of that matters when companies have to cut back.

Even though working at *El Diario* hadn't been my dream job, I had been happy with what I was achieving and everything I was learning.

I had been able to convey to my boss the importance of growing on the digital front. I purchased my own little recording device and microphone so I could start creating content. I came up with the idea of a digital show where I narrated the newspapers' most important headlines and columns. I called it *"La Semana, Nueva York"* ("The Week, New York") and shot it myself in iconic places around the city. I would place my tripod in the middle of a street and do my own standups—that's what we call the reporters' on-camera presentations or commentary. (Sometimes I needed a plastic fruit crate to literally stand up on since I'm so petite. *Hola*, props!) In my free time, with the help of Ana Maria, I would edit the whole thing down to ten minutes.

It was much more work than what my job description entailed. But I wanted to absorb everything and fulfill the dream I came from Venezuela to chase.

Looking back, I realize I was a YouTuber before it became a thing! I was not the best camerawoman or the best editor, but I learned the basics of shooting and editing. I didn't stay home thinking, *Will I make it to TV one day?* I pitched innovative ideas that were easy to execute and that made the company look good.

My everyday job consisted of writing stories. But since I wanted to be on TV, I pitched my bosses at *El Diario* stories to record on camera, edit, and post on their website. That's how I came up with the idea of pitching an entire webcast.

Twitter was also starting to attract users, so being the youngest employee with knowledge of social media, I volunteered to learn about it and teach courses on it for the newspaper writers. I even helped some of the older folks there set up their individual accounts.

All this required more work for me, sometimes staying up late or working weekends, but it was worth it.

The executives at this newspaper, like managing editor Alberto Vourvoulias-Bush and publisher Rosanna Rosado (now New York governor Andrew Cuomo's secretary of state), were thrilled and encouraging.

I also learned to always think about the needs of the one you're pitching to. Pitching is everything in journalism; it's raising your hand and telling the coach you're ready to be put in the game; it's not waiting for a story to be handed to you, but rather bringing the stories you care about to life.

But pitching is hard. I've had a ton of good ideas that never made it off the starting line because I couldn't get editors interested. I still struggle with this today.

What's the one thing that helps? Again, it's the power of a story.

A good pitch is like a bedtime story rather than a school paper. "Once upon a time . . ." is engrained in our psyche, after all. And it starts with knowing what your bosses are into, then reading up—not only the national newspapers but the local ones—to find strong stories and characters. In about half a minute, you pitch an idea that encompasses what the story is, who the voices are, one or two sources, any relevant data, and the time and place.

Journalism requires investigating those in power, but also, as Masha Gessen, a staff writer at *The New Yorker*, put it, journalism is telling people about other people.

I pitched stories to my bosses and to executives in other departments. I learned to have pitches on the tip of my tongue so that if I ran into an executive or editor at the elevator, the bathroom, or even a holiday party, I could sell them. I was determined not to let the limitations or guidelines of my current job determine my future. When we work with what we have, we can make it a stepping-stone for where we want to go.

After many months, my boss congratulated me on my little web segments, and when he needed a reporter to work Saturdays to read the newspapers' headlines on our paper's allied Univision station, channel 41, he asked if I was up for it.

The publisher had set up a tiny camera from Univision 41 in the middle of our *El Diario* newsroom. I had to get up in front of all these staff writers clicking away in their computers on deadline, put on a mic, and speak up.

I wouldn't get paid more. I kept my same job description. But I had one minute on TV every week.

Sixty seconds that I cherished more than anything.

I even came up with a closing line so the audience would remember me: "*¡No te lo pierdas!*—Don't miss it!"

After a couple of months, many viewers remembered my catchphrase. I was on my way!

The day of the firing, thinking about my small successes gave me enough strength not to break down or complain in the hallways. I was going to get through this setback.

Now I am convinced that getting fired made me stronger and helped me grow a thick skin. You have to know: no one, absolutely no one, is indispensable. That's why it's so important to have a plan B to fall back on, a work alternative—along with a good support system of family, friends, and a spiritual community. Hopefully it never happens to you, but if unemployment knocks on your door, it doesn't have to be the end.

When I got to the little space inside the library I shared with Ana Maria, the dark-suited individuals were talking to her.

"Mari, they want me to keep working here, doing your job without pay!" she blabbered in front of them.

I stopped breathing for a second. I couldn't believe it. This was like pouring salt on my wounds.

"It would be an opportunity for me to stay here, and I don't get paid anyway, but . . . I'm going with *you*," she declared bravely.

I exhaled. I wasn't alone. This was my *Jerry Maguire* moment, and she was my Renée Zellweger.

"*We* are leaving together," I told them matter-of-factly.

Before we left, I quickly called a lawyer. He said the firing would definitely cancel my visa papers.

The knot in my throat grew bigger.

I had thirty days to find another job that would sponsor my visa—in that terrible economy—or I would become undocumented or have to return to Venezuela. This was not a good alternative; crime and crisis there had worsened. None of the options were viable.

I put myself in the shoes of so many immigrants who struggled to get papers and keep their status. As I left, I promised myself I would commit to telling the stories of what it means to navigate our obsolete immigration system. I would speak for those who have to embark on that journey with fewer resources than I had.

Hearing experiences like mine firsthand is the most effective way for anyone—from both sides of the aisle, Republican and Democrat—to understand how outdated the system is and that there's a real need for comprehensive immigration reform. If someone like me, who had a job and a graduate diploma from an Ivy League school, could become undocumented *in one day*, what about everyone else?

After I wrapped up with the lawyer, Ana and I picked up our belongings and made the long walk from the library to the elevator. The hallways were lined with glass conference rooms, from which employees looked at us with discomfort or pity, as though we were walking a plank on a pirate ship.

"Wait!" Ana said suddenly as we got to the elevators. "I left something."

"Oh my God, Ana. What?!"

She ran back in, and when she returned, she was holding the bag of light pudding snacks.

"*Chama*, if we are going to be single, undocumented, *and* unemployed, we've at least gotta be in shape."

The elevator doors closed.

I saw the "Seriously?" on her T-shirt and burst out crying.

#*Go like Mariana*: Most of us won't get to the top by riding the elevator; we will have to take the stairs. But we will relish that staircase, the journey. If you have to start from the basement, don't get discouraged. Just think: the view from the top will be that much sweeter.

7

The Yes Attitude

New York City, 2011

Oh man, I'm not going to get to the airport on time!

The piles of clothes around me were a reflection of my mental state. My NYC–Miami flight was departing in an hour and a half. Since I was moving to a new city to start a new job, I had my entire life in suitcases.

The truth is that I purposely left the packing till the end, to avoid getting too sad about leaving New York.

It had been a year since I had lost my job at *El Diario*, and a new chapter of my life was about to begin. Which meant more goodbyes. Uprooting. Starting from scratch. Again.

Leaving Venezuela, where I lived for twenty-four years of my life, had meant leaving my home, my family, and my friends. And even though in New York I had gone through plenty of professional ups and downs, after three years I had finally managed a certain emotional stability and a group of friends.

After I was fired from the newspaper, I spent as much time as possible over the next couple of weeks looking for jobs that would sponsor immigrant visas, an almost impossible task in the Great Recession of 2008 and 2009.

A lawyer suggested one of the ways to avoid becoming undocumented (save from marrying an American or buying an expensive investor visa) was enrolling in school again, so, for the time being, I went back to Columbia for a part-time master's degree in Latin American studies.

I felt it was unfair for my family to have to pay another semester at college. My dream was to work to help my people in Venezuela, not have them help *me* out! What once seemed like a meager salary plus health insurance from *El Diario* now seemed like a dream.

My parents always used to say every lesson is a valuable one. But this was a lesson I would have traded in an instant.

"*Mi* Mari, *yo sé*, I know it's a financial sacrifice," Papi had said over the phone. "But we have our savings. We will support you. We've always said studying is an investment, something nobody will ever be able to take from you."

As a child, year after year, I would see Mami with her *letra cursiva,* filling out long applications in perfect cursive for us to attend summer camps and schools in the United States to learn English. The discipline paid off. I ended up being valedictorian in high school. In my speech, I thanked our parents and friends, comparing them to the winning ticket in a lottery. To show my appreciation to all sixty of my classmates, I made fake tickets that I printed and cut out one by one at home. All the pieces of paper had the same number. We were all winners. Whatever we did with our golden tickets was up to us.

That's why that setback in New York was so difficult for me. At twenty-six I didn't want to study anymore and acquire student loan debt for me and my family. While all my classmates from Columbia seemed to be on their way to success, I was wearing a school backpack again to keep my legal status in the US. That backpack symbolized my failure.

It was tough for me to grasp how this had happened. I had done everything right. Every day I thought about how hard it was to stay in the US legally. *What is an immigrant supposed to do if he or she gets laid off or fired? What if someone can't find a job fast enough or can't afford to pay for school or an investor visa?*

By then I had decided I was going to use any platform available to lend my voice to as many of the eleven million undocumented people in America—and the millions more who were here legally, fighting to make it—as best I could.

Even while I was back studying at Columbia, I kept recording my little videos around the city with my camera and tripod. I did interviews, attended events, and even edited my own news stories for a small public television station called Vme-TV.

"*¿Puedo entrevistarlo?*—Can I interview you?" I asked one of my new professors, Patricio Navia, who taught Latin American Politics at NYU.

He agreed, and when the interview ended, he gave me a straightforward word of encouragement: "You have so much talent."

"But I can't find a job," I told him.

Patricio, "Pato" as people called him, was a powerhouse. He was a Chilean political scientist who knew everything about Latin America, and he also was a respected newspaper columnist. I had decided to take his class at the last minute—a crossover class at New York University—and I barely made registration.

Logistically, taking Pato's class didn't make much sense for me because I had to dash out of Columbia and get on the subway all the way from 116th Street on the west side to 14th Street on the east, at rush hour. I sat down out of breath every day.

But I had a feeling in my gut. This man was a human bridge, like me. And I wanted to learn from him.

"*Yo te voy a ayudar*—I'm going to help you," he said one day out of the blue.

An acquaintance of his had just gotten a job at Univision Network, the Spanish TV giant, and he said they could probably use a smart girl like me on the team. Pato, whom I never would have met if I hadn't gotten fired, helped me get that big job interview.

Soon I got a callback and flew to Miami. Unlike many immigrants from South America, I didn't know Miami well; I hadn't been there in years. I also had never driven in the United States; when I lived in NYC, there was no need. Back in 2011, Uber didn't exist in Miami; cabs were very expensive, and the drivers took cash only. So I had to muster the courage to rent a car to make it to the interview.

"*¿Estás loca, mija?*"

Mami was going bonkers over the phone.

"Are you crazy? You're going to crash, Mariana del Carmen. You were a bad driver down here in Venezuela to begin with. Remember, it's not like it is down here in South America, where traffic lights are a suggestion—the cops up north don't kid around with traffic signals."

She made such a fuss about it that I told her I was having a friend pick me up.

And then I got in the rental car, made the sign of the cross, *me persigné*, and on I went.

At our meeting, the talent director for Univision News pulled no punches. "Forget about being on TV. What we can offer you right now is a job filling digital content. The position would be here in Miami."

After earning my one-year master's degree from the journalism school, getting laid off, going back to school, and taking on irregular gigs here and there, it was time to tackle new horizons. I hit the pause button on the Latin American studies program and took a leap of faith.

I said yes.

In New York, Ana helped me load up my bags in the car. She hugged me and said, "It's the end of an era. I think you're a grown-up now, *chama.*" She laughed out loud, turned around, got on her scooter, and disappeared into the Manhattan skyline, just like Peter Pan going back to Neverland. I was left to face the real world.

As the cab went down Fifth Avenue, we passed by the iconic 30 Rockefeller building, home of NBC News. I pressed my face against the window and sighed.

All the English network headquarters were in New York. But I hadn't made it through the door. Not even close.

One day I'll come back here, I thought, looking at 30 Rock. *And I'm going to work right there.*

A three-hour flight later, I was landing in my new home.

Miami, 2011

Miami was a scene of nightclubs, palm trees, traffic, and building cranes. It was slowly coming back to life after the recession, with the help of thousands of Brazilians, Venezuelans, Colombians, Cubans, and many more who reached its shores.

I had never lived in the so-called US capital of South America, but I quickly fell in love with its blend of accents, colors, and cultures. And because I'd be better off performing brain surgery than attempting to cook, I loved how easy it was to get *arepas* in almost every neighborhood.

In a couple of days I got a Florida driver's license (not an easy task with my driving skills) and I showed up at my new job—admittedly filled with insecurities.

I didn't have any experience writing or creating this kind of digital content, much less for such a large news site.

When I was taken up to the area where I would sit, which the digital department shared with the news show *Primer Impacto*, I noticed we were a very small team. Only a handful of people to fill up the entire Univision News website! This included the immigration section, op-eds, United States politics, and news from around Latin America and around the world. *Geez, esto sí está del carrizo—*this is going to be tough.

But hey, at least I had a cubicle! And the boss seemed nice and willing to teach me.

"Can we go grab a coffee?" he asked. "I want to tell you more about the dynamic around here."

When we arrived at the coffee shop and sat down with our drinks, I thanked him for welcoming me. But this wasn't a casual coffee meeting.

"There's something you should know," he declared. "There will be cutbacks, and I am leaving for CNN. This is my last week with the company."

The Hispanic TV giant had also been hit by the recession.

I put my *cafecito* down because my hand had started trembling. I tried to sound calm. "Excuse me?" I asked.

"It is what it is. We thought that since you're young, you could actually do the job of several people. There will only be a couple of folks left in the digital team."

My new boss was leaving for greener pastures while he could.

But within a week of my arrival, other people would be laid off without warning—just as I was starting. It reminded me of what had happened to me a year earlier. I felt guilty. Vulnerable. Uncomfortable. Even though it wasn't my head on the chopping block, I was worried I would crash and burn while trying to carry the team and be fired all the same.

Remember when I told you to always have a plan B in case you get fired or face a professional setback? Well, at this point I was still learning that lesson.

When we left the coffee shop I had to find a place to vent. I didn't want people in my new office to see how upset I was, so I drove to a nearby parking lot.

There I sat, petrified. I tried to count. I tried to pray. But the only thing that came out were tears of fear and frustration.

In order to move to Miami, I had rented an apartment and leased a car for an entire year; I had taken loans to buy furniture. And there was the critical issue of my visa, which Univision had sponsored for me to come on board.

Ana Maria was right. This was a crash course in "adulting," and there was too much at risk. *What did I get myself into? What am I going to do for this move to work out?*

No matter what, I had to avoid getting fired again; otherwise I could become undocumented.

I returned to Univision with my eyes puffy and swollen.

And then I spotted her. Her hands and arms were filled with shoe bags, an outfit change, and her purse—and still she managed to walk with such poise! She was on her way to record two of her shows, her wardrobe in tow.

She had the most recognized female face in Spanish news and the grace of a woman who doesn't need to impress anyone. It was María Elena Salinas.

Something made me get out of the car and go after her. I managed to catch up with her at the front door. I opened it, and she kindly thanked me with one of her megawatt smiles.

I followed her inside, telling her how much I admired her and how excited I was to meet her. Her ease encouraged me to keep going. We walked all the way up to her office, and she hung the clothes she'd been carrying in a little closet. With absolute naturalness, she invited me to sit down.

Her stunning face was framed by her daughters' drawings on the wall behind her—another powerful reminder that women have to wear different hats all the time. It doesn't matter if we work at home or in an office, we are always expected to give our best. No days off.

MES (her acronym, as her colleagues know her) had a career spanning more than thirty years and had won dozens of awards and acknowledgments for her trajectory. I got lost staring at that straightforward gaze I had seen so many times on TV. And I saw why she had won the trust of millions of Latinos who watched her on *Noticiero Univision* night after night.

She was the same person who sat on the anchor chair, with the same voice, the same dignified gestures, and her most extraordinary quality—her willingness to share her knowledge.

With genuine interest, she asked me about my goals and experience. I couldn't believe someone so important was taking the time to get to know *me*.

I will always remember what happened next: María Elena Salinas gave this whippersnapper reporter one of the best pieces of advice I've ever gotten.

"Say yes to everything that comes your way. Later in life, you'll learn the power of no, but for now, say yes to every opportunity," she urged. "Even if it's not exactly what you want to do or if you feel you can't do it, just have *the yes attitude*."

My time was up. She had to read her scripts and get ready.

Kindly, she concluded, "Ah—and my door is always open, Marianita."

I went to my desk a changed woman.

That night I stayed up late filling all the digital content for the website. And in the morning I even dared bring my little camera and tripod. I was going to say yes to everything. I wanted to stand out in my job and also try to get on TV to help so many immigrants like me.

Univision was the place to do it. Univision Network is one of the top networks in the US regardless of language and the most-watched Spanish-language broadcast television network in the country, available in more than 80 percent of US Hispanic households. It embodies the voice of the Latino community and consolidated the most iconic stars under one roof: Don Francisco, Cristina Saralegui, Jorge Ramos, and María Elena Salinas herself.

Both Univision and Telemundo don't just fulfill their missions of informing and entertaining the Hispanic audience; they also shape the identity of Latinos in the United States, with an extraordinary intimacy to our people, many of whom rely on these networks for immigration advice.

The next day I arrived with a ton of energy, but I soon realized I was very poorly dressed for our office environment. I saw a parade of celebrities with elegant shoes, outfits, and accessories. The bosses wore traditional suits, and the producers sported a creative mix of designer and casual pieces, all on trend.

This was TV, baby! I had arrived with a wrinkled skirt and a shirt from the Gap. I felt like Cinderella with no fairy godmother.

This oldie but goodie is as valuable as ever: "Dress for the job you want, not the job you have."

Still, I tried not to feel intimidated. Even though it was noisy and packed with people, I set up my tripod and camera in the middle of the intake room, a NASA-type control room with a bunch of computers where engineers and producers gather video from all over the world. I took a deep breath, stood in front of the camera as if no one else were there (as I had done so many times before in the much smaller newsroom at *El Diario*), and recorded one of my segments to upload on the website.

When I finished, I noticed María Elena was outside watching.

"Marianita, you're not bad overall," she said, "but watch your posture and tone of voice. You tend to slouch, and your delivery is way too fast. I suggest you take on a voice coach—I have a good contact if you need it—and try to think of how you want to project a look that reflects who you are, while always thinking about your audience."

That night in my newly rented apartment, I made a decision that most likely changed the course of my career. I was going to ask María Elena Salinas to be my mentor.

María Elena responded by practicing what she preached: she said *yes*!

Even though we didn't have a formal pact, every time I approached her for advice, she welcomed me with open arms and an open heart. To this day I consider her one of my closest professional confidantes.

No one gets far alone. From JLo to blogger Chiara Ferragni, and even the Kardashians (who've proven to be very able businesswomen), those who are successful all have people who guide them, like human compasses. It's essential to identify a mentor to guide you along your journey—preferably someone older than you, in your industry, who understands what you are going through. Build your team and nurture it throughout the years. With them by your side, you'll be able to face any battle.

I had managed to get the most valuable piece of the chessboard on my side, a true queen!

And I needed all the help I could get.

I spent many months doing the job of several people. I created digital content. I recorded it myself with my equipment for the site. My supervisors even started asking me to shoot company events. I didn't think it was beneath me. I said yes to absolutely everything. I thought it was the best way for people to get to know me.

That's how I ended up being spotted by the head of the TV news division, the respected and very well-known Colombian journalist Daniel Coronell. He asked around, and people said, "That girl can write, shoot, edit, and be on camera. Oh, and she says yes to everything."

Ina Mazzei

This is the map of my world. Let's start our journey!

At my happy place in La Guaira, Venezuela, at age five, with my sister, Graciela (four); my brother, Alvaro Elias (one); and Mami.

Papi drops us off at summer camp in Minnesota, far away from Caracas.

My siblings and I sightseeing in New York with the Twin Towers behind us. Years later, I would witness 9/11.

Finding the courage to be myself at the beach club's pageant.

Graduating from Columbia University and really scared about what the future would hold.

Venturing out with a camera for the first time, as my friend snapped this pic.

Interviewing Eva Longoria on live TV at the Democratic National Convention in 2012.

With my mentor and trailblazer, María Elena Salinas, who always calls me "Marianita."

On the set of *Good Morning America* with Lara Spencer, George Stephanopoulos and Elizabeth Vargas, and my cohosts, Yannis and Pedro. It was my first time on English-speaking TV.

Lou Rocco/ABC via Getty Images

Mariana Atencio

I asked the king of Spain to take the first selfie of his life. The photo went viral and broke the internet.

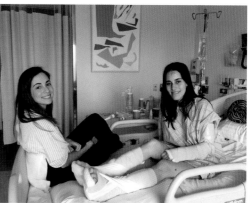

My family's life came to a screeching halt after Graciela's accident.

Diana Atencio

Mirna Couto

On the set of *Noticiero Univision*, the signature news show watched by millions of Latinos across the US.

Mi amor popped the question on a paddleboard in the middle of the ocean!

My sister and I enjoying a day at Central Park after her recovery. We always have each other's backs.

Papi didn't just walk me down the aisle; we danced to Stevie Wonder's "Signed, Sealed, Delivered (I'm Yours)!"

Giving my first TEDx Talk, called "What Makes You Special?" So far, it has been seen by more than eight million people worldwide.

Attending the White House Correspondents' Dinner, feeling miserable after I had been told, "Please don't look too Latina."

The following year I went back with the most colorful gown, this time being perfectly me.

Peter Shaw

At the epicenter of one of Mexico City's most heartbreaking earthquakes, reporting for MSNBC.

Peter Shaw

Covering the migrant caravan as it made its way to the US in 2018.

Anthony J. Scutro

On the set of MSNBC's flagship show *Morning Joe*, speaking about what it means to be an immigrant.

Reporting the aftermath of one of the most devastating hurricanes in Florida.

Peter Shaw

Our last vacation together in Tulum, Mexico, a month before Papi was hospitalized.

Jose Torbay

Jose Torbay

We spread my dad's ashes in Venezuela, his home country, and New York, the city that he loved.

Eleven years after the mountain climb where I was held at gunpoint, I went back to conquer my fears.

Univision wanted to launch an investigative unit, a team dedicated to in-depth research on drug trafficking, corruption, immigration, and political scandals. Gerardo Reyes, the prestigious Pulitzer Prize–winning investigative journalist, was to lead the venture. And Coronell asked me to join.

I was a newbie whom everyone at Univision now referred to as Marianita.

To tell you the truth, I was scared. *What can Marianita bring to the table next to Coronell and Reyes?* I knew I wasn't ready for a job like that. I had never even done an investigative report. Honestly, it wasn't something that interested me at that point. Plus, they also clarified they weren't going to raise my salary, and my title would remain "Associate Editor, Digital."

But I thought about what María Elena had advised.

Who knew? This was going to be a trial run, after all. I exhaled and said yes.

I spent almost three years at *Univision Investiga* with amazing professionals who took me under their wings. Often the tasks were frustrating, like reading through depositions or driving for hours to personally convince a witness to cooperate with our investigation. I even went on stakeouts—which aren't nearly as exciting as you think from watching them on TV. (There's a lot of eating in the car.) But I tried to do everything that was asked of me.

As it turns out, it was very special to be a part of something we started from scratch.

From my colleagues I learned to hold those in power accountable, to always look for different ways to tell a story, and to value the importance of perseverance.

When I first started at Univision, I wanted to be on TV every day and travel around the world chasing breaking news, but here you had to sit your butt down and look through mountains of paperwork and video to discover *one clue*—usually a tiny one—nobody else had noticed. Like when we investigated a Latin American politician who claimed to adhere to communism, but I found a social media video of a lavish party he threw for his daughter's *quinceañera*.

Consistency, discipline, and the yes attitude bore fruit and gave me the first big achievement of my journalism career.

It was a detailed investigation into a gun-walking program—where the US government purposely let illegal guns be sold so they could track them—called "Operation Fast and Furious" (yep, just like the movie). Our work involved finding weapons sent to Mexico by the US government, which the Obama administration had apparently lost and had ended up being used by narcos to kill hundreds of people. The American government reportedly placed rigged RadioShack tracking devices on the weapons; when the trackers failed, the weapons disappeared.

We found more than thirty. We—a small, bilingual investigations unit—brought to the table something the bigger outlets and their huge teams couldn't. We didn't have their resources, but we did possess a unique knowledge of the border and Mexico. So when other networks stopped tracing the guns after they went south, we persisted. We actually found the guns in crime scenes in Mexico and tracked them back to the US.

Thanks to our unique knowledge and access in Latin America, we found these weapons.

A person familiar with the congressional hearings called Univision's findings "the holy grail" that Congress had been searching for. With a TV special titled *Fast and Furious: Arming the Enemy*, we won a Peabody Award and an Investigative Reporters and Editors Award, two of the most prestigious in journalism, and firsts for Univision in 2012. I was part of the first team to accomplish this at the network.

I had a platform and newly found confidence in my ability to do my job.

Winning a Peabody Award was an unbelievable success for my young career. It had happened thanks to the gravitas and experience of the head of the news division, Daniel Coronell. It gave credibility and respect to a unit that was in its incipiency. We had beat the English-speaking legacy networks for the most prestigious award in journalism.

I tried to bring what I learned from that experience to every project after it. Two years later I wrote and anchored a documentary about press freedom in South America called *PRESSured*. For a year and a half, I followed journalists from six countries—Brazil, Mexico, Cuba, Venezuela, Ecuador, and Argentina—to document how they were condemned and silenced, their lives threatened for doing their jobs.

That could have been me, I thought in every instance. I needed to keep fighting to tell their stories. For that project I later won a 2014 Gracie Award from the Alliance for Women in Media, a national organization that recognizes "exemplary programming created by women, for women and about women."

The stories that impressed the awards committee were about two brave women defying those in power. One was Yoani Sánchez, a dissident journalist from Cuba, who chronicled the everyday failures of the Cuban regime. *Time* magazine had listed her as one of the world's 100 most influential people in 2008, stating that "under the nose of a regime that has never tolerated dissent, Sánchez has practiced what paper-bound journalists in her country cannot; freedom of speech." I interviewed Yoani by a stroke of luck during her first trip to Miami in years.

I also followed Delvalle Canelón, a female reporter from Globovisión (a small opposition news station in Venezuela), as she covered the military during the presidential election. Delvalle was harassed by the equivalent of a four-star general in front of his troops for doing her job. President Chávez later gave that military commander the highest honor you can bestow on a soldier, essentially rewarding his behavior. Delvalle's life had been made a living hell ever since. (She now leads the national journalists association.) I was able to bring her story to a mainstream audience in the US.

Investigative reporting was beginning to give me hope that justice was possible—and the awards told me people were listening. For me, the drive to bring these stories to life blurred the line between professional and personal.

My next big assignment would be my most personal yet: an investigation unmasking corruption in the Venezuelan government, for which I was nominated for a national Emmy Award.

I went to Venezuela to investigate Chávez's inner circle. I went into the barrios where many of these now-powerful men started, and I uncovered aircrafts, sports cars, and mansions acquired from a web of corruption and drug trafficking. This was a long-form segment for a *60 Minutes*–type show called *Aquí y Ahora*, which María Elena Salinas coanchored.

After years of feeling guilty for having left my loved ones behind, I was finally doing something to help my country!

I asked Papi to come with me to the News Emmy Awards ceremony at the Time Warner Building in New York. I was given only one ticket, but at least he could escort me to the elevator.

I didn't win, but remembering everything I had been through to get to that elevator was the best reward. Seeing my dad drop me off at the most coveted ceremony in journalism, wearing my cocktail dress and feeling like his little warrior princess, was a dream come true—for both of us.

That night he reminded me of the advice he gave me when I told him I wanted to be a journalist in his study in Caracas: "You have the tools to develop the passion you have inside. Work hard. And remember to always be yourself. Authenticity and tenacity are what prevails."

I needed that type of encouragement to do what I had set out to achieve: be on screen to inform and empower our community.

A turning point in my mission came in the 2012 presidential campaign, thanks to Luz María Doria, executive producer of Univision's morning show, *Despierta América*, which is the Spanish equivalent to the *TODAY Show* and *Good Morning America*.

Luzma is more than a boss at *Despierta América*. She truly believes in developing the talent that comes through her studio.

Despierta América is a byproduct of her vision. She pours her heart and soul into those four hours of live TV every day, and countless hours after, when the cameras are off.

That year, Luzma needed a reporter who could go to both political conventions to do live hits—live shots offering the audience commentary from a location where news is happening.

I doubt I was among the first people she thought of. I hadn't done live TV, much less for a morning show. But that day someone else had asked if I would introduce Jorge Ramos at a political town hall with Republican candidates, and of course I said yes.

Often opportunity will knock on your door unannounced. If you're not ready with the willingness to try (that yes attitude), the diligence to do your homework, and the desire to learn as fast as you can, it's possible you won't even hear the knock.

I had never covered US politics. Truthfully, I didn't even know exactly *what* a convention was or how it worked. The ordeal was harder than I thought. But I studied hard and got through the Republican National Convention, which came first. It was an eye-opening experience that taught me much about the way US democracy worked. I met delegates from all over the country and saw women I admired, like former secretary of state Condolezza Rice. That first convention went by in the blink of an eye. But for the second round, the nerves got to me. I was much more aware of the gravitas of what I was setting out to do.

On the morning of the Democratic National Convention, I woke up at 3:00 a.m. to get through the exhaustive security detail surrounding the long list of VIPs, among them former presidents, senators, and celebrities. Since *Despierta América* goes on the air at 7:00 a.m., there wasn't a minute to waste.

My job was to be live in front of the podium as the stage was being set up and preview who would give speeches that night, their talking points, and the overall importance of the convention.

Campaign coverage is like the World Series of news. The English-speaking networks invest millions of dollars in preparing their convention coverage, which lasts for weeks. Hispanic networks, having fewer resources, still make a great effort and send several teams. This was a really big deal.

I had opted to wear a multicolored jacket because I wanted to stand out with some Latino flavor in the sea of grays and blacks, the usual shades of choice for people who cover politics.

The first day of the DNC meant new faces, talking points, and a different agenda to memorize. I was supposed to go live again with no script and no prompter. An hour before going on air, I started to worry. I had survived the first convention, but what if I made a mistake before finishing the second one?

I started to count as I inhaled and exhaled. Everything I had succeeded in doing in the past few years meant nothing as I stood alone on a cold convention floor at 6:00 a.m. It was as if my mask of security fell off to reveal the scared little girl who had gotten fired from the newspaper and was a digital nobody. Marianita.

"*Uno, dos, tres* . . . And we're on the air in half an hour." My crew was setting up the cameras in front of me.

Oh God. I felt my hands sweat and my knees tremble.

I need something or someone interesting for this live hit. I panicked as I looked around me.

In that moment, I spotted my life jacket. Eva Longoria, the celebrated actress from *Desperate Housewives*, was rehearsing to make her political convention debut speaking on the importance of the Latino vote that night on the main stage.

She was the only high-profile Latina in that space at that hour of the morning. This was not a coincidence. I had seen her rise in Hollywood, and witnessing how she was becoming a political force gave me courage.

It took me ten minutes to get to her. She was all the way on the other side of the convention floor, which was the size of a concert stadium, but I ran over so I wouldn't lose my chance. I asked for a live interview, and as soon as she said yes I signaled to the cameraman. When the camera light went on, I started talking, visibly nervous.

My questions were very stiff. I was tense. Luzma, the executive producer, was watching from the control room all the way in Miami, but I hadn't heard a peep from her. No "great job" or "good get." Nada. *Shoot!*

While Eva answered my questions, my mind kept racing, thinking about what I could do to lighten the moment. Even if it was a political segment, I was interviewing an actress for a morning show.

I looked to the floor and saw that Eva—who is petite like me—was wearing the biggest platform heels I had ever seen, and they made her considerably taller.

"And lastly, Eva, can you tell our audience about your shoes?" I smiled and kept going. "I'm sure a lot of women watching at home want to know your secret."

She burst out laughing. The cameraman panned to the floor and focused on the shoes. The audience went wild.

Luzma finally spoke to me through the IFB (an earpiece through which the director of a show communicates with you while you're on live TV). In her radio voice she said: "Marianita, you're going to be big."

Not only did I cover both conventions that year, but months later I ended up coanchoring part of the election results on Luzma's morning show.

I shone on live TV—on the ground and in studio, talking to all sorts of people. I had found my sweet spot. Investigative reporting had been very gratifying and will always be a part of my wheelhouse, but being on the scene for the biggest stories of the year, representing my people on a daily basis, experiencing the rush that comes with unpacking headlines and providing context—this was my purpose.

But when the 2012 campaign cycle ended, I started feeling insecure again. What was I going to do now? Go back to digital? Investigations? I had nothing solid. My official title still read "Associate Editor, Digital."

At this point in my life I learned that I needed to keep saying yes, but I also needed to start thinking of what my next step would be. Look for opportunities, and grab the ones that come knocking on your door.

Later in my career, I understood this also means saying no to things that seem important but aren't the top priority. We tend to want to do it all, but it can dilute our efforts. *"El que mucho abarca, poco aprieta,"* as Mami says—Jack of all trades, master of none.

At that time, though, I still wanted to do it all. I was desperate to see what the next stage of my career would bring. Patience is not one of my virtues. But I didn't have a choice.

A couple of weeks later, as I was walking in the same parking lot where I once cried, a Univision executive came up to me with a question I wasn't expecting: "I have seen your work. You're good. By any chance, do you speak English well enough to be on camera?"

Turns out, Univision had just partnered with none other than Mickey Mouse—Disney, in other words—to launch a cable network for multicultural Millennials called Fusion. Because of my age and background, the multimillion-dollar project was a perfect fit for me.

The executive told me there were auditions *the next day* for the female host of their morning show, and I should just show up.

I was reluctant and doubtful, but I couldn't let this opportunity pass by. So the very next day, I was on site.

I wore a fuchsia button-down shirt tucked into an A-line flower skirt. The audition was held on the set of *Sábado Gigante*, Don Francisco's iconic show. This wasn't a demure news set by any means.

The people auditioning included cartoonist Lalo Alcaraz, White House spokesperson Gaby Domenzain, and politicos Matt Haggman and Fernand Amandi, among others.

I was told about the panel of judges that would be reviewing the tapes: the president of Disney-ABC, Ben Sherwood; the head of ABC Talent, Barbara Fedida; and the head of ABC News, James Goldston, among others.

Whoa, Dorothy, you're not in Caracas anymore.

I was told to sit on a couch with other talent and have discussions around different topics, while the cameras were rolling. There was no script. I took a deep breath in, and I was off. I could only be real.

Fast forward to October 17, 2013, when I found myself on *Good Morning America*, and the rest is history.

Like all the amazing things that had happened since I received that email about my scholarship to Columbia, I knew this also had God's handwriting all over it. Though I often felt overwhelmed by the tasks in front of me, I was slowly learning that the yes attitude meant showing up and doing what needed to be done, however imperfectly, with authenticity.

And people were responding. Stories were being told. The hope that I would finally be able to be a bridge between people on TV was growing within me. All those differences I'd once found frustrating were beginning to morph into unexpected strengths, keeping me afloat in a sea of new challenges.

#*Go like Mariana*: No one gets far alone. Build your team and nurture it throughout the years. With them by your side, you'll be able to face any battle.

#*Go like Mariana:* Used well, the yes attitude can take you to places you never thought you'd go. Where could the yes attitude open doors for you?

8

Riding the Wave and Crashing

Miami, April 10, 2014

I felt on top of the world. I was driving to the studio in Miami to host our morning show on Fusion.

I looked at the recently applied white nail polish on my hands as I swerved onto the freeway. I was pretty sure Jose, my boyfriend of two years, was going to propose sometime soon. He was everything I ever wanted: sweet, smart, supportive, and also an immigrant from Venezuela. We'd met in Miami, where he worked tirelessly to create jobs and build his own business. Plus, he had that Latino look with a dash of Lebanese that made my heart melt.

I was lost in my thoughts, thinking about what kind of a wedding we would have, when I got a call from my parents.

The situation back home in Venezuela had gotten worse. I had begged them and my sister to come to the States and get away for a little Easter break in New York City. Jose and I were going to join my family in the city that weekend. He later told me he was planning on proposing then, but it was not to be.

"*Hija*, are you on the air?" my parents asked.

I immediately knew something was wrong. "What happened?"

"It's your sister, Graciela. She's been in a car accident."

I felt my heart stop.

The words made no sense: "It is unlikely she will ever walk again" and "life-threatening injuries."

She had been hit by a car in New York City. A hit-and-run accident.

Everything around me became blurry.

"We are on our way to the hospital," Mami sobbed. "*Tu Papá* will speak to the police."

I couldn't hear my parents' voices anymore.

"Nooooooo!" I screeched inside my car.

My heart jumped into full panic mode. It pounded so dangerously fast and loud I thought it was going to burst inside me. I lost sense of where I was or what I was doing.

My hands were shaking as I gripped the steering wheel and managed to pull over. All I could hear was my heart and the whooshing sounds of the cars going by at high speed. It was the first and only time I've ever questioned reality. I was convinced it was a nightmare.

It wasn't.

Everything had changed in a split second.

A part of me had been in that car accident too. All I knew for sure was that my sister needed to see me when she woke up. I needed to be there for my other half. I needed to get to New York as soon as possible.

New York City

During the three-hour flight, all I could do was pray, my face pressed against the seat in front of me.

Por favor, Dios, save her, I implored. *If you save her, I promise you we will get through whatever other challenges we have to face. We will get through it as a family, but please don't take her from me.*

When I got to New York Presbyterian in Manhattan's Upper East Side, my parents were in the lobby. They hadn't been able to see her yet. Admittedly, I felt a selfish relief. I wanted to be there when Graciela opened her eyes.

Soon we were allowed to go back to the ICU. That image of her lying on a hospital bed—with a surgical collar and wires hooked up around her body, her raven hair all crusty from the dried blood, and the beeping noise of the anesthesia and other medications dripping into her veins—haunted me for a long time.

She could barely speak. But when we locked eyes, we became like mirrors shining back at each other. We had seen one another at our weakest. But we knew it would be okay—because we were together.

Without knowing exactly what happened, she had a look of determination.

I'm going to make it through this, her eyes said to me.

I am going to make sure you do, mine told her.

There's something about the certainty of having someone else in the world who can see you at your best and your worst but loves you anyway that makes you feel invincible, even if you're tied down to a hospital bed.

The doctor lightly touched Graciela's body with a medical pen to determine if she was going to be able to walk again.

"Do you feel this?"

She nodded.

"Do you feel that?"

She nodded again.

Both legs. Saved.

I exhaled and put my hands together in prayer.

Thank you, God. Gracias.

He had answered my prayer. Now I had to keep my promise. And what lay ahead for us was no small feat.

I leaned on my younger brother, Alvaro Elias, who also made it to New York from Colombia, where he lived and worked. Though Venezuela's crisis had scattered our family to different places, this accident brought us back together to face another kind of challenge.

Graciela spent five days in the ICU. Those first few days are a blur to her. She was highly medicated and slept all the time.

Looking at her broke me.

She had casts on both legs; the bones in her feet were practically pulverized from the accident. A cast on her left arm. A giant scrape on her forehead with dried blood. More scrapes on her nose. Metal bars around her pelvis because it was fractured. The possibility of internal hemorrhaging, which is common in high-speed accidents, still threatened her life.

After the first few days, she was sent to a step-down unit. It still wasn't a regular room at the hospital, but she had improved enough to get out of intensive care. This would be home for the next several weeks.

This was when reality started sinking in. Through the fog of medication, she began to understand she'd been in an accident. The car had hit her left hip, and the impact threw her in the air. Apparently, she had landed on her feet and then had fallen to the ground. As a result, she fractured her hip, pelvis, and left arm. But the worst were her feet, which had multiple fractures. The foot and ankle contain twenty-six bones (together making up one-quarter of the bones in the human body). They hold our entire weight!

I couldn't help but think back to when my sister and I were little, how Mami was *sobreprotectora*, very overprotective. We never got into enough trouble to have stitches, casts, or even cavities. Ever. Neither of us.

I only remember one time we even drew any blood. When we

were five and six, we went to play every afternoon at a park in Caracas with a little creek running through it. One day I declared I would hop from one side of the creek to the other. Naturally, my little sister said she wanted to do it too. Even though Mami dressed us the same, at that age a year's difference was very noticeable between Graciela and me.

We both ran toward the water. Deep down I knew her shorter legs might not make it. But I didn't stop her.

Graciela jumped behind me. She hit her head on a rock at the ledge of the creek. There was blood all over her face.

Surprisingly, since she also landed on her hands, the injury wasn't bad enough for stitches. The doctor ended up gluing her forehead together with some sort of Latin American super glue.

Mami was furious.

"*No cuidaste a tu hermana*—You didn't take care of your sister. Look at the hole on the girl's head!"

Since then Graciela has a little dent where her hairline meets her forehead. Only I see it, and only I really know how it happened.

I was thinking about that dent when Graciela's primary trauma doctor came into the room. The young orthopedic surgeon explained to us briefly that he would perform many surgeries in the next couple of weeks. They would start with an internal fixation of her pelvis. (The day she was admitted they had only performed an external fixation, he said.) Then they'd operate on her left arm; it was in a cast but needed screws. And eventually when her feet were less swollen they would operate on each foot separately.

All I thought about were Mami's words during that first fall in the creek—a premonition that somehow brought us here to this hospital in New York City.

No cuidaste a tu hermana, I kept repeating to myself. *You failed to take care of your sister.*

On top of everything, we didn't understand half of the doctor's words or, even worse, their implications. Even though my parents and I spoke English, the terminology and approach was cold and alien to us.

Coming from South America—where *el doctor* is most likely your dad's *amigo*, where the staff were likely your friends and neighbors and the environment is warm and informal—we found navigating the health system in a big city like New York to be a huge culture shock.

New York Presbyterian is a teaching hospital, so every day countless different doctors would enter my sister's room and discuss her case with their students or residents. (Yes, just like in an episode of *Grey's Anatomy*.) They would ask her questions from her chart, discuss some things with her nurses, and then leave. The process was so impersonal, and it angered me. It was as if Graciela's feelings didn't matter. During my travels as a journalist, many families tell me they're also scared and confused when navigating the complicated health system in the United States.

In addition, dealing with international health insurance was a nightmare. The whole process was frustrating, and sometimes my family and I felt the hospital was just interested in our insurance money.

But it was how this would profoundly change Graciela—physically and emotionally—that daunted me the most.

Most of the time she was in a lot of pain and very uncomfortable. She has always been afraid of needles and blood, so she barely moved for the fear of pulling one of her many catheters.

"I can't feel my legs," she moaned over and over. The anesthesia numbed them, but not enough to make her pelvis stop hurting. Any slight movement was excruciating.

Being in bed for so long gave her a lot of time to think. The more she learned about her surgeries and their consequences, the harder it was to imagine a full recovery.

"You will need to learn how to walk again after we fuse the subtalar joints in your feet," the doctor told her. "Eventually, you may walk with a cane or a walker. But you won't be able to wear high heels again."

This last phrase hung over her like a dark cloud.

"After everything I've been through, I know I shouldn't focus on that," she confessed to me, "but it takes away from how I see myself."

Since Graciela was a lawyer at a high profile firm, the everyday dress code at her office included pencil skirts, fitted blouses, and heels.

We have brains and hearts, but many women—especially Latinas—place a lot of value on our appearances. It is a big part of our personalities. As much as my sister and I were straight-A students and hard workers, Mami taught us that—along with eating properly at the dinner table and saying *"por favor"* and *"gracias"*—taking care of ourselves physically and working out were also important.

At that moment we realized, once again, Mami was always

right. Graciela's fitness level helped her recovery a great deal, but at first she could barely move. She did not have the strength to sit up straight in bed without help or to sign her name with her good hand. She could not move her legs and depended on nurses changing her position every hour so she would not get bedsores.

After the car crash, her old life was over. She went from being a workaholic who missed Christmas the year before to no longer being able to use a computer. For a time she was angry at everything and everyone.

"Instead of feeling grateful for being alive and surrounded by my caring *familia*," she told me once, "I am especially angry at God."

But she never stopped trying to get better, even if the goal for the week was just to bend her legs a little bit or move a few inches in bed by herself. She kept at it even when every effort was exhausting and painful. I honestly don't think I would have been half as resilient.

"In my mind," Graciela told me, "I will only be happy the day I start feeling like my old self."

She was accustomed to planning everything. She wanted to know the exact date she would be able to go home and resume her old life, but it was a question no one could answer. The worst parts were the uncertainty and coming to terms with the fact that she was never going to be her old self. The accident forced her to shed all material things and focus on what was really important.

For me, everything I had accomplished thus far suddenly evaporated, as if it had happened to someone else. My sister and her struggles were front and center.

Things had changed. Our lives were upended. Graciela and

I had always been on parallel paths. Now there were challenging physical differences between us, changes that would affect us forever.

Those differences would be immensely painful. I had to make sure this person I loved unconditionally knew that despite shattered bones and shattered dreams, she could make new plans and create a life that would fulfill her.

Suddenly, life divided into two eras: before the accident and after the accident. The world before felt like another dimension.

We were told that Graciela's initial recovery would take at least six months to a year, and that following her discharge she would need to be bedridden for three months before she could stand on her feet.

I divided my time between New York and Miami as best as I could. Back at the network, I would get to work at 4:00 a.m. Research. Smile. Read the prompter. Every time I saw Jose after work, I would start sobbing uncontrollably, refusing to believe what had happened.

I also found comfort not only from my closest friends at Univision but also from people like Barbara Fedida and Ben Sherwood, who both called me upon hearing the news. Barbara kindly continued to follow up. (She still asks me about my sister to this day.)

The mind is a powerful thing, and it only took a couple of minutes of what-ifs to pull me deep inside a dark tunnel. *What if I had been there that day? What if I had called her five minutes before? What if it had been me and not her?* For everything Graciela was going through physically, I was living a mental nightmare. Now I can compare it to the "upside down" from Netflix's *Stranger Things*.

But in the world outside the nightmare, life seemed to go on. *The Morning Show* certainly did.

Every day I did two hours of live television on Fusion. I got to interview people like Tyler Perry, who never forgets his roots; Cameron Diaz, who is funnier than many of her characters; and Pierce Brosnan, who is a true gentleman and photoshopped male perfection.

Engaging in everyday morning banter for a young audience also meant my cohosts and I got to be ourselves on the air. Millennials and Generation Zers do not want cartoon-like "broadcast people" on screen. As Papi said, authenticity is what sticks with people, and ultimately what feels good.

Just days before Graciela's accident I had celebrated my thirtieth birthday on TV, and my team surprised me with Brazilian *Carnaval* dancers. Their outfits were so skimpy the producers had to quickly attach the feathers on their heads to their behinds!

As soon as I spotted the dancers on set, I jumped up from my anchor chair and started dancing with them live on the air. I was back at *Carnaval* in Venezuela.

After Graciela's accident, though, my emotions plummeted more than I thought I could bear. Seeing her suffer so much altered my sense of time. Each day felt like a week, and each week like a month.

My sister had five surgeries in her first five weeks in the hospital. Most of the surgeries lasted hours and took a toll on her body. She had barely recovered from one procedure before she had to undergo another one. She was losing weight really fast and was always nauseous and weak from lying down all the time. But her journey was just beginning.

Weeks after the accident, I got the news that I had won a Gracie Award from the Alliance for Women in Media for the documentary on press freedom in Latin America. The irony was not lost on me. One of my sister's nicknames is Gracie, short for her beautiful name, which suits her perfectly since she is the most graceful person you can imagine.

Gra, Gracie, or Gacho is the person you can always count on. The one you call when you need life help; the one who always remembers to get Mami a birthday card or to bring you groceries from the supermarket because you've been traveling nonstop. She's the one who stayed home to take care of our parents and put her dreams on hold. She's gracious about everything she does for you. She makes you feel as though you are the most important person in the world.

Gracie is our family's gravitational pull because she's always helping one or several of us at the same time.

For me, going to the Gracie Awards was a big deal. It meant attending a black-tie event in Hollywood, getting up on stage to receive the award, and giving an acceptance speech. I should have been so excited. But I felt as if this were a test I wasn't ready for.

Remember when I told you to build your team, because no one gets anywhere alone? I called in my squad. I asked my mentor, María Elena Salinas, for advice on the speech. A friend made the dress. Another made the earrings. I went with my colleague, Spanish journalist Tomás Ocaña, who made the documentary with me.

I tried to enjoy the moment. But half of me wasn't there. I was riding the biggest wave of my career and crashing at the same time.

That night I sent my family some photos, trying to lighten the mood. I quickly regretted it.

Here you are all glammed up while they are miserable in some hospital room. You messed up, Mariana! I said to myself.

I felt the urge to go see my sister—immediately. She was the only thing that mattered. I left the award show, booked a last-minute red-eye flight on my phone, and dashed from the party to the airport, picking up my bag on the way. In a public restroom I stuffed my lavender dress into my carry-on, changed into a pair of black slacks and a T-shirt for the flight, and put my hair in a ponytail. I didn't even bother to wash my face.

Every minute, every mile closer to her, I grew more certain of the need to do this. I almost felt that if I made it to her that night, she would somehow magically get better.

Seven hours later I walked into New York Presbyterian in my sneakers and smeared makeup. I looked ridiculous, but I needed to get to Graciela.

Then I heard a voice I knew all too well, distorted with chilling screams that could be heard all the way down the hall. They were unmistakable. They were my sister's.

I ran down the hallway, dropped my carry-on at the nurses' station, and opened the door to her room. She was screaming in pain.

Thankfully she wasn't alone. Mami's sister—*la tía* Lucia—had flown in from Caracas for the week to help out.

"*Tía, menos mal,* thank God you're here! Gra, what's wrong?"

For days, Graciela had been complaining that her wrist was hurting. It turned out it was also fractured, but no one had noticed.

The hospital staff had been almost entirely focused on her pelvis and feet.

I assumed the anesthesia had waned. We called for help. The nurses gave her some meds and proceeded to put a cast on it.

After a couple of hours, I could tell she was feeling better because she started poking fun at me.

"Are you trying to bring back the smeared mascara trend?" she said.

"Wait, look at this," I replied.

I pulled the hair extensions from my toiletries bag. My blonde *tía*, who is kind of a clown, put my pieces atop her own head, like a toupee, grabbed the Gracie Award from my carry-on, and pretended to be me, thanking the academy.

We all burst out laughing.

But deep down I was so scared.

My midnight visit from across the country helped raise my sister's spirits, but I didn't know what else to do.

Graciela finally left the hospital, but she couldn't go back home to Venezuela. She had to officially quit her job at the law firm and stay in New York because she still required more surgeries and treatments.

How were we going to finance all this? My little brother stepped up. As an economist, he helped Papi rearrange our family's finances to pay for all the physical therapy and extended stay in the city. We were a tribe. I knew it then; my siblings were the best link to my past and the people most likely to stick with me in the future, as director Baz Luhrmann put it.

Like most New York apartments, our family's place has small rooms and bathrooms. Graciela's wheelchair didn't fit in the bathroom and barely made it through the bedroom corridor. So she spent most of the next three months in bed and only went out if she had a medical checkup. Nurses visited her for round-the-clock care.

"This is so hard, Mari," she told me with tears in her eyes.

But no matter what, she always showed a willingness to overcome her circumstances. Over time, she started going to physical and occupational therapies daily and then had additional therapy in our apartment in the afternoon. She lost so much muscle mass she could barely stand up with a walker. But she persisted. I admired her more every minute.

She repeatedly told me she couldn't have done it without my parents, who put their lives on hold and moved to New York to care for her long-term.

With the help of the hospital, the US government gave the three of them visas for medical reasons, until Graciela was off all her pain medications, blood thinners, and treatments. But they couldn't leave the country or they would lose their status.

At first Mami had a hard time coping with the situation. She tried to hide it, but I became aware of her distress when, for the first time ever, she didn't know what to cook for dinner. I caught her frozen in the kitchen, where she had always been a master.

Papi was the little bird flying above the fray. He would spend hours each day in Graciela's room, helping her with physical therapy. He would strap small ankle weights to the casts on her feet and make her lift her legs. He encouraged her and cheered whatever progress she made.

But the doctors in New York weren't optimistic. Graciela's feet were getting worse instead of improving. Then came the terrible news that her foot surgeries had not been successful; she needed additional reconstructive surgery. Apparently her bones had not healed as expected, and she had what doctors called a malunion.

Graciela even started looking into amputation.

My parents refused to give up. Saving her feet became their mission. They went to every appointment and consulted with different doctors for second and third opinions.

They rolled her wheelchair to Central Park in the afternoons so she could get some fresh air. They also insisted she come to church with them every Sunday, though she never agreed. At this point in the process, my sister didn't really want to talk about her feelings and also needed time to reconcile with her faith.

Then one day, out of the blue, she said yes. I remember Papi tried not to make a big fuss about it so she wouldn't change her mind. They rolled her wheelchair to the Church of St. Vincent Ferrer on 65th Street, which was closer than St. Patrick's. Graciela wanted to sit in the back and be out of sight. She told my dad she didn't want to take communion. She felt guilty about having turned her back on God.

The priest noticed Graciela in her wheelchair all the way in the back of the packed church. He slowly came down the aisle, knelt before her, and said, "The body of Christ?"

"Amen," she replied, and opened her hands for the host.

What happened next was nothing short of a miracle.

Some weeks later, at the worst point of her desperation, Graciela found out about a doctor in West Palm Beach who ran the Paley

Orthopedic and Spine Institute, a limb-saving clinic. This doctor was a leader in reconstructive orthopedic surgery and specialized in patients with bone and joint conditions. Graciela wrote him an email about her story, and he answered within a few days.

My sister became convinced Dr. Paley was the only one who could help her. Choosing this doctor was not an easy decision. It implied packing up and moving to Florida, renting a place to stay, since my apartment in Miami was too small, and leasing a car. But she was determined.

In the course of the next year and a few months, my sister went on to have a total of seven surgeries at the Paley Institute.

It was completely different from my family's experience at the big New York hospitals. The doctors were very warm and called Graciela by her name. They gave us a better, more hopeful perspective about her situation. The halls were mostly filled with kids who had all kinds of conditions. Physical therapy for adults was done in the same room as the children's, decorated with colorful pictures and balloons.

Graciela started being much more active in her recovery. She would quiz her doctors and therapists for hours. She started seeing friends more often and joined a group of women who made rosaries for poor Catholic communities in Central America. She even joined a gym to work on her arms and chest while in her wheelchair.

"For the first time in my life I am only focused on the present," she told me, "on making every day the best possible."

The truth is, finding yourself in a wheelchair at twenty-nine definitely makes you different—the kind of different that makes others stare and feel sorry for you. Oh, the pitiful stares! It was tough to deal with the way people looked at her, looked at us, everywhere we went.

During our traumatic ordeal, I learned that sometimes it's hard to find a positive in certain differences. My sister is not better off because of what happened. If I could do anything, I would turn back the clock and prevent the accident. But Graciela taught me that you can't let a limited notion of others define you.

Being able to reimagine yourself beyond what others see is probably the hardest task of all, but it's also the most beautiful. It allows you to create your better self.

Graciela never returned to her old job at the law firm. She doesn't really care about material things as she did before. To this day, she lives a more purposeful life. Now she's started her MBA and wants to go into nonprofit work. In the end, she went from being the one who needed us to being our biggest lifeline, the one who always pushes us to be better.

As a family, we've become closer, turning to each other for support and moving forward together. We appreciate the simple things. And our hearts break more easily for those who are suffering.

I'm proud of how my sister carries herself. It's as if she's been beaten up but is still standing taller than me—taller than all of us. I'm proud of how she shares her story and approaches the world with vulnerability and strength. Proud of how she goes to the gym and works out harder than anyone else there.

Graciela is on her feet now, but her recovery isn't over. She continues to make progress every day. I remember what Papi taught us about resilience, the human ability to adapt and overcome gracefully. She embodies it.

#Go like Mariana: Being able to reimagine yourself beyond what others see is probably the hardest task of all, but it's also the most beautiful. It allows you to create your better self.

#Go like Mariana: No matter what people see—labels, stereotypes, or differences—you decide what you allow to define you.

9

Paddling Through Happiness

I've shared a lot about where I came from, the places where I grew up, the experiences that modeled my values, and the challenges and fears that have taught me my biggest life lessons. But because I'm a woman, and specifically a woman in the media, many ask me about the infamous work-life balance. As I said before, women are constantly trying to wear multiple hats and battling to have it all: an exciting and fulfilling career, a stable relationship, kids, good friends, a savings account, a solid Instagram game, less cellulite—catch my drift? It's an impossibly high bar, and it can get exhausting fast.

I was always a go-getter academically and professionally. But in the love department? That's a different story. Perhaps it's because South American society is rather conservative when it comes to relationships. Or maybe it's because I went to an all-girls Catholic school—love seemed to have a lot of rules and imposed expectations.

I have a confession to make: I was scared to get married.

I'm obsessed with watching Hollywood movies, and I had started to see myself as Julia Roberts in the Garry Marshall films. I was either Julia in *Pretty Woman*, telling myself, *It's okay to want to be rescued. It's okay to want the fairy tale. I want Richard Gere to come get me in his red convertible, bouquet in hand, screaming "I love you!"*—or I was Julia in *Runaway Bride*, galloping away from her beloved on horseback in her white dress.

It's not that I was a commitment-phobe. Quite the opposite; I was a serial monogamist. Much like Julia's *Runaway Bride* character, Maggie Carpenter, I would wholeheartedly give myself to every relationship, molding myself depending on the person I was dating.

Rocker dude? I was into Nirvana and Pink Floyd and wore dark-colored shirts for an entire year.

Jock guy? I was into baseball games and hosted our Latin American version of a tailgate while decked out in his team colors.

Film director? I organized casting sessions in my home and literally picked up the electrical cables from the floor and counted the money for his movie projects.

But after a while, I would snap out of it. Put on my sneakers and run. *À la* Julia.

Why? I was running away from my own bluff. Mariana the rocker chick, or the sports nut, or even the film assistant were creations that didn't hold up. As much as I valued being real in my work, it took me a long time to see that I wasn't being real in my personal relationships.

In hindsight I see that the same fears and limiting thoughts that came up about not being good enough at work also reared their heads in my relationships. I pushed people away by not being brave enough to love while being myself.

Sometimes it takes learning to love and accept yourself first before you can really open up to another person.

When I met my husband, Jose, I was coming off one of my phases of pretending to be someone I wasn't. It was a moment when I didn't need a boyfriend. I actually wanted a friend, which is why I didn't have my guard up.

Miami, 2011

In 2011, I had just moved to South Florida for the job at Univision. New to the city, I felt like an immigrant in every sense of the word (yet again), and after the stint at the newspaper in Brooklyn, I had no job stability. I feared I would get fired again. But I was about to make a connection that would change all that.

I was lying out by the pool one day with my new neighbors—girls from home whom I knew well.

"Did you know Jose Torbay is getting divorced?!" I overheard one of them saying to her friend.

"I told you his marriage to that *mexicana* wasn't going to work," the other replied as she sipped her lemonade.

"To add salt to the wound, he just quit his job to launch some startup. Now he's alone, out of a job, and back at his parents' house," the first one added.

As much as I love my *paisanos*, my countrymen, many Venezuelans and Latin American transplants in the United States find it difficult to open their hearts to people who don't come from the same social background. It's a feudal mentality that hurts all of us. It feels as if you are in the same village you grew up in, surrounded by closed-minded people who feel entitled to a privileged status just because they have the "right" family name.

Even though they were at a beautiful pool with the Miami skyline in the back, these women were still in Caracas.

I didn't know who Jose Torbay was, and I didn't care. But I remembered his family lived closed to mine back home, and I wanted to help.

"The guy probably needs a friend right now," I replied.

"You're right," one of the girls acknowledged. "I might invite him over to play tennis."

"You should come, Mariana," the other said as they both splashed some more Australian Gold on their butt cheeks.

Even though I didn't think much of it, I did play tennis. I'd learned the sport at summer camp in Minnesota. I thought it would be an easy way to socialize in the Sunshine State. So I signed up for what ended up being my first date with this Jose.

Well, at least an attempt at it.

The day of the match came, and I was heading out of the Univision newsroom, sneakers in hand, when someone yelled, "Mariana, we need you to log some tape."

No, no, no . . . this can't be happening, I said to myself.

But I couldn't say no. Being the digital reporter with *the yes attitude* meant sitting back down and transcribing word by word the thirty-two-minute interview. This was going to take some time.

Ugh. I didn't even have Jose Torbay's number to cancel on our doubles match.

I was a no-show and felt awful.

Jose later confessed to me that after his tough divorce, he had been looking forward to meeting me and was actually decked out in his best tennis outfit. (He doesn't play regularly, so in retrospect, I doubly appreciate the effort.)

That night I looked him up on Facebook to apologize. When his profile pic come up, my eyes widened.

OMG, he's so cute! I said to myself. *And he probably hates me.*

It took me longer to figure out what to write on his Facebook wall than it had taken for me to transcribe the entire half-hour interview at work.

"Dear Jose," I wrote. "It's a pleasure to meet you . . ." (delete, delete) "a pleasure to e-meet you."

¿Mariana, qué es eso?—What is that? This isn't a work email. I sound so dorky.

"Jose, I am so sorry I couldn't show. I am a journalist and it was a breaking news situation . . ." (delete, delete).

Does transcribing an interview qualify as a breaking-news scenario?

Hmm, well, it was needed for news. Who is to say what really constitutes "breaking news"?

"Jose, I am so sorry I didn't show up for the tennis match today. I am a journalist and it was a breaking-news situation."

In my desperation to make friends in this new city, I added, "I'll be having ceviche with some people downtown on Friday if you want to come."

"Some people" constituted my colleague Tomás (my one friend at work) and Maria Valentina, a friend from home. But after all the stress at Univision, I was looking forward to going out for the first time.

Who cares? This cute dude probably isn't going to show up anyway.

I didn't hear back from him and figured he probably never wanted to see me again.

That Friday, the casual Peruvian joint Ceviche 105 was popping. My two friends and I were chatting away at a booth when I spotted him.

Jose was at the door, all alone. I gasped. Even though our families lived a couple of blocks from each other in Venezuela, it was the first time I had ever seen him in person.

He looked like an Olympic diver. His skin was the color of cinnamon—a combination of the Caribbean and Middle Eastern tan. His salt-and-pepper hair reminded me of George Clooney.

I'll confess: I am usually not into good-looking guys. But he seemed kind of shy, not even aware that he was handsome, embarrassed to be there but making a big effort anyway.

He glanced at me and waved with a hint of a smile. He walked all the way down the corridor of tables until he made it to our booth.

We both kissed on the cheek (as it's customary among Latinos, even if you are meeting for the first time). I felt a little electricity go down my spine.

"*Gracias* for waiting for me," I said.

"Always," he replied.

The tone for our relationship was set.

Jose has gotten used to waiting for me. Literally, as in the tennis fiasco, and figuratively, as he gives me the space I need to do the job I love, while showing unconditional support.

That first night he quickly changed the subject, asking if I knew how to dance salsa. I laughed and said, "Let me show you."

We said goodbye to my friends and went to Mango's, a South Beach tourist staple that plays salsa and merengue music. It was the perfect place for our first nonverbal communication. He is a natural. His body flows with the music as if it is coming from within.

He took the lead smoothly. The arm tension was just right, the footwork always landing on the perfect spot, as if we had danced together a million times before. We were both amazed at each other's precision and kept doing turns and changing moves from mid- to fast-paced to challenge our ability to adapt. My whole body was tingling. The feel of his hand holding and releasing my waist while subtly guiding the next move was addictive. We were gliding across the room.

It was love at first dance!

When we finally sat down to talk, I was utterly impressed with his charm, his intelligence, and those eyes that showed such a beautiful soul.

We started dating with the same ease we found in the music.

The girl on the dance floor was the real me. I found my life partner because I was relaxed. When I embraced who I was and wasn't playing a role, it simply happened.

Even though Jose hadn't even been divorced a year, he was convinced I was the woman for him. He took me as his official date to his sister's wedding six months after I stood him up for tennis.

"Are you sure you want a steady relationship so quickly?" I would ask.

"Of course. I know what I want. And it is you," he always replied.

Dealing with being divorced wasn't easy for him, because he believed marriage lasts "until death do us part." But after two years, he felt ready to propose to me.

He had been hiding the ring in his sock drawer for months, but Graciela's accident changed the timing of his plans.

After talking it over with my parents, sister, and brother, who were totally supportive, Jose decided to go for it. He would attempt it over the Fourth of July break in 2014. We were supposed to spend the holiday weekend with my family and my sister in New York.

But as often is the case, my work found a way to wedge itself in. A few days before we were set to go to New York, I was asked to be a substitute anchor of Univision's national newscast, *Noticiero Univision!*

The main anchors were either on break or headed to the border to cover the 2014 child migrant crisis, which had exploded over the summer. Since Fusion was partly owned by Univision, and the studio where I hosted my own show was just a few steps away from the *Noticiero* studio, I was an easy stand-in.

I went to the studio the weekend before to practice. One of the tech guys turned the lights on for me. I wanted to rehearse and get familiar with that space. I was so nervous.

I am a big believer in overpreparedness. Create your content. Study the audience and stage. Preplan your outfit. Control the predictable factors so you can be nimble for the unpredictable ones.

Sitting in the chair of my mentor, María Elena Salinas, was a big deal. Anchoring for an entire week meant informing millions of Hispanics and immigrants across the country—and fulfilling one of the main goals I had set out for myself when I almost became undocumented. It was a career high while dealing with a personal low, my sister's accident.

I was torn. When I told my family I'd considered passing on this opportunity in order to be with them, they said, "Absolutely not. You need to do this. You need to sit in that anchor chair." They were able to watch me from the apartment in New York. They texted me photos beaming with pride. I missed them, and I was filled with mixed emotions.

Jose was understanding, generous, consistent, and rational. He is the perfect balance to my impulsiveness, my desire to push myself too hard or undertake too many things at the same time.

The weekend came and went. We were building our relationship, which became a solid rudder.

In the time we had been together, my entire life—my family, my home, my work—had turned upside down. You see, falling in love on the dance floor is easy; growing in love when the music stops takes work.

On his shoulder I was slowly finding a new home and learning what love was really truly all about.

After my sister's accident, almost every day I saw Jose, I would lie on his chest and cry my eyes out. I cherished the moment when our breathing synched up, his heartbeat encompassing mine. Pain would wane.

I felt safe.

Two weeks after the Fourth of July, Jose convinced me to drive down to Key West, where he had booked a beautiful hotel suite, saying that we needed a little time to ourselves. I thought it was a good idea and didn't think much about it.

When we arrived at Casa Marina in the Keys, the lady at the check-in counter seemed confused.

"Mr. Torbay, there must be some sort of mistake. I don't have your reservation for today. It was actually booked for yesterday," she said nervously.

Jose's tan skin turned pale.

"¿Qué, qué?—What?" he replied, checking his phone in disbelief that he had booked the wrong date.

I didn't get why he was so rattled. We checked online for other options. Almost all the nearby hotels were booked.

"Why don't we take a walk on the beach while we wait and see if something opens up?" I suggested. We already had our swimsuits on from the long drive down, thinking we might stop to swim on the way or jump in the water when we got there.

As we strolled the packed beach, I could sense Jose's uneasiness. He later admitted he wasn't going to propose surrounded by strangers with coolers, listening to DJ Snake and Lil Jon's "Turn Down for What."

All of a sudden he spotted a pair of paddleboards and a creative solution to his dilemma.

"Let's rent them!" he cheered. I gladly agreed since it seemed to make him so happy.

We went so far out into the water, we couldn't even spot the beach. It was just the two of us in the middle of the ocean.

Jose started wobbling on the paddleboard.

"*Loco*, what are you doing?" I asked without realizing what was happening.

He got on one knee on top of the board and pulled out a ring from his swim trunks.

"Mari, you are loving, courageous, passionate, funny, and the woman I want to spend the rest of my life with. You bring out the best version of me. I want to save that for you."

As he looked up at me, his big, brown eyes caught a reddish shimmer from the sunset. His tanned skin glimmered with salt water. Since we were in the middle of the ocean, the only thing we could hear was our breathing.

This was my fairy tale come true.

"Will you marry me?" he asked timidly.

There was no urge to run. To swim away. To jump off the

board. Instead, I was overcome by a sense of joy, peace, and certainty. I didn't need anyone or anything else.

"*Mi amor*, yes, a thousand times, yes!" I screamed at the top of my lungs.

More wobbling.

"But please," I said, "let's put that ring on right away, because if we fall from this paddleboard and that thing sinks, I am going to have a heart attack!"

We laughed. Floating in the middle of the ocean, I knew I had found my soul mate. In my mind, the birds and fish cheered us on, and it couldn't have been any better.

That night I thanked the Lord and secretly asked him for a miracle: "I want my sister to be my maid of honor."

I also told Jose about it, and he said he would help in whatever way he could.

Team #TorbayAtencio was formally born.

A couple of weeks later the lease on my apartment was due to be renewed or terminated. I didn't know what to do. The landlord was going to raise my rent, which I couldn't afford, and I didn't have enough time to look for a new place.

Jose surprised me by asking if I would consider moving in with him. At first I thought about my family values. In Venezuela, as in most Latin countries, moving in together *before* you actually get married is still described as "living in sin," so I could only imagine all the unsolicited advice I was about to receive if I decided to go through with such a decision.

Some of my classmates back home regurgitated urban legends about *una fulana*, an unnamed girl who had moved in with her man and ended up pregnant and alone after living together for a year. But most importantly I was afraid I was going to hear about it from our church and my close family.

"*Mija*, why buy the cow if you can get the milk for free?!" I heard from my *tía*.

Ay no. Anything to avoid this *cantaleta*, the constant nagging I would never hear the end of.

If Latinos are conservative, Latino-Lebanese like Jose's family are all the more so. There are many Arab and Jewish communities in Latin America, and they share our values of tradition, family, and liveliness too.

Jose's own brother and younger sister, whom I both love and respect, never lived with their partners before tying the knot. But Jose was already a divorcée, and that gave him the maturity to understand that this time around he wanted to get to know his bride before placing a wedding band on her finger.

Like his family, all of our parents and friends who live in the motherland are much more traditional than those of us who have moved to or grown up in the United States.

There is a point where others start saying that *you are not Venezuelan enough* (insert whatever other nationality here—Mexican, Colombian, Cuban) if you adopt what are considered "American values" too quickly. (Although it's true that in many communities in the States living together is still considered scandalous; in others, people can't imagine why it would be a big deal.)

"Mariana, you've become a *gringa*—Americanized," a good friend said.

"Oh *Dios*, what if your *abuela* finds out?" my other *tía* said. "She's going to have another heart attack!"

I was a working woman, an adult, but I didn't want to disappoint my parents or give Jose's family the wrong impression about me. I felt caught between two cultures, not belonging to either world.

I asked Jose to give me some time. As usual he understood and allowed me to do what I considered best.

Mami, who's the most conservative in my family circle—but also the most pragmatic—gave me the soundest advice. "Mari, I know you are navigating through a lot. This hasn't been an easy year for our family. But something I've learned is that love heals everything, bridges every gap, and is the only foundation for a good marriage like the one *tu papá* and I have," she said. "Do you love Jose?"

"Yes, very much," I said firmly.

"Then follow your heart and forget about trying to please everybody else. Do what you want to do; that's all that matters."

We moved in together the next month. My mom reminded me that it wasn't about how other people saw us in some idealized version of their reality; it was about our real life in the real world, the home, and the future we were building together.

I did ask Jose to wait to get married until my sister was strong enough to attend the wedding and actually have a good time. That required more waiting.

One day Graciela finally told me she was ready. "I will do it for you, for me, and for our family and friends who have shown me the greatest love and support."

On my wedding day—October 24, 2015—after enduring fifteen surgeries in two years, Graciela walked down the aisle as my maid of honor.

It was an enormous trial. She had undergone a surgery just two weeks before; she still had to wear walking boots and needed a wheelchair to get around.

We slept in the same bed the night before my big day, with the lights off, cuddled up against each other, like when we were little and shared the same bedroom.

"I can do this," she whispered.

"And I want to see you do it," I replied. She smiled.

The next afternoon hundreds of our guests from around the world waited in anticipation at Miami's Fairchild Tropical Botanic Garden. The music stopped as Graciela, in a beautiful cream-colored dress that hid her walking boots, stood up from her chair at the end of the aisle and put one foot in front of the other.

She was in pain, but she didn't show it. Her smile was so bright, her elegance beaming, the radiance of her achievement so overpowering that every single one of our guests felt the weight of the moment.

My dad and I watched from a little balcony up the stairs with tears of joy. We were so happy, we decided to dance down the aisle! Why not? God had delivered our miracle!

Papi and I danced to Stevie Wonder's "Signed, Sealed, Delivered," and our friends and family started clapping.

The priest couldn't help but say, "What an entrance!" on the microphone as everyone took their seats.

It was there, before our family and friends, knowing that everything was as it should be, that I made a commitment to the man who had held my hand through it all.

The lyrics to the song for our first dance, Juan Luis Guerra's merengue "Ay Mujer," said it best: "Love is the beginning and the end. Your love gives me wings to soar above the sea."

Jose promised to focus on our home, our fur-balls, our *peluditos* (goofily what we call our future kids), and on being happy together—our life project. We'd seen how healing and being real was bringing new life all around us.

Six years later, balancing the unpredictability of the news business, my professional ambitions, and our relationship has been challenging, but it has also been so beautiful.

When Jose and I met, I was a reporter who constantly feared getting fired, and he was launching the company of his dreams. We are both protagonists and witnesses of each other's American dream. It's a bond we share. But we also have shown each other every part of who we are, our strengths and weaknesses. And we continue to choose each other daily. In the end, that's what it means to grow up in love.

#Go like Mariana: Love heals everything, bridges every gap, and is the only connection strong enough to make every relationship work. Be relentlessly real in all areas of your life, personal or professional. And remember, the first person you have to love and accept is yourself.

10

A World of Separation

Homestead, Florida, November 2016

"Will I ever see my mom again?" a wide-eyed, eight-year-old girl named Angelina asked as she tugged on my dress.

Donald Trump had just become the president-elect of the United States. It was election night in 2016, and I was on the air for NBC News. Almost a year to the day after our wedding, and just two months into my new job at NBC, this was my first big assignment in English after crossing over from Spanish.

Political teams at the networks prepare for a night like this for several years. I'd come on board in the home stretch of the presidential election that redefined American politics. I wasn't going to make it on the air with the regular content, so I pushed to do something unexpected: I pitched to be live, watching the results with dozens of undocumented families.

"Lester, you sense the anxiety in this room," I told NBC News anchor Lester Holt during our network election special. "Some people are holding hands. They even held a prayer," I added.

Although many journalists interviewed undocumented people, no other English-language network understood the groundbreaking importance of featuring this type of watch party side-by-side with more traditional ones. After all, undocumented immigrants were among those that stood the most to lose that night. Almost all the children in these families were American citizens.

"Is Mr. Trump going to deport my mom now?" Little Angelina started sobbing as our broadcast continued.

"It's going to be okay," I told her as I hugged her tightly and managed to get her to smile. But I honestly didn't know for sure.

We were live for almost twenty-four hours that day. When we wrapped, I had a sunken feeling. Even my team said I needed to get my energy up for the next round of live hits in the morning.

I couldn't stop thinking about Angelina.

This girl was around the same age I was when I went to camp in Brainerd, Minnesota, and she already knew she was "the other." She understood her family was different. She walked home from school in fear. Her mom could be taken any day.

Donald Trump based his candidacy on painting us as "the others," to be feared and deported.

"When Mexico sends its people, they're not sending their best . . . ," he said as he announced his run for the Republican nomination at Trump Tower in Manhattan. "They're bringing drugs. They're bringing crime. They're rapists . . ." It set the tone for so many other instances of xenophobia that frankly wouldn't fit in these pages.

On November 8, 2016, Donald Trump won the presidency by racking up the 270 votes needed in the Electoral College, while losing the popular vote to Hillary Clinton by almost 2.9 million votes. It became clear a big part of the electorate didn't understand who "the others" were.

Some saw people coming to take their jobs or potential terrorists who speak a different language. On the contrary, many minority groups saw intolerance, hatred, and narrow-mindedness from the other side.

The Trump presidency changed everything for us immigrants. Within the first week of taking office, he attempted to implement a travel ban that targeted Muslim countries that would eventually be struck down by a federal judge. ICE (Immigration and Customs Enforcement) raided many businesses for being suspected of employing undocumented immigrants, and Trump deputized local law enforcement in communities across the United States to moonlight as immigration officers.

His administration also changed the mission of the US Citizens and Immigration Services (USCIS), desisting from "securing America's promise as a nation of immigrants" to "fairly adjudicating requests for immigration benefits while protecting Americans, securing the homeland, and honoring our values." USCIS also changed its processing times for those wishing to emigrate legally—an act widely criticized by immigration advocates.

Little Angelina knew what was in store for her family. She sensed the fear in her mom and others around her.

Just like in my native Venezuela, where polarization grew to a point where it destroyed us, in the post-2016 US we found ourselves stuck in political bubbles no one was willing to burst. The problem is that polarization not only fuels deep divides of ideas; it fuels policies that eventually have devastating effects on families as a whole. It breaks them apart. I could not know, looking at those frightened children on election night, that our family would feel the sting of separation just months later.

Caracas, April 2017

"Mari, *por favor,* I need you to get down here now!"

Mami called me in a panic. Her voice trembled as she told me she could smell tear gas coming into our apartment in Caracas. For months, hundreds of thousands of people from all walks of life had taken to the streets to protest against the authoritarian government. Violence and political repression in Venezuela had reached its highest levels, coming to a peak in May 2017.

After almost twenty years of a failed revolution led by the late Hugo Chávez and his successor, Nicolás Maduro, the country's economy had collapsed, resulting in widespread food and medicine shortages.

Medicine prices skyrocketed, as well as those for food and other basic goods. The International Monetary Fund estimates inflation will soar to 13,000 percent before mid-2019. Perhaps what was most telling this time was that people were descending from the slums, which had historically been a Chávez stronghold, to protest. Now the whole country was not only fed up but hungry.

I didn't even see this coming when I decided to leave after college; it seemed unbelievable that an oil-rich country couldn't even feed its own. To add insult to injury, Venezuela was now the most dangerous country in the world for the second year in a row.

The government security forces responded violently to the protests and stripped the opposition-led parliament of its powers. More than one hundred people, mostly students, died during the unrest. Some were gunned down in the middle of the street, their murders witnessed by thousands on social media feeds. By this point, independent outlets had disappeared.

My mom started crying on the other end of the phone. She feared for my dad, who would attend every single protest shoulder to shoulder with the students risking their lives. I could see him with his Yankees hat and worn-out sneakers. "If we don't stand up and fight for this country, who will?" he would say.

My younger brother, who would have been marching alongside our dad, left several years before it got really bad. He worked in the oil sector in Colombia, with all the Venezuela émigrés from that industry. So Mami feared especially for my sister. Graciela could not have a promising future down there. After completing her recovery, she had returned to Venezuela with my parents only a few months prior. After everything they had done for her, putting their lives on hold until she could walk again, she vowed to take care of them, refusing to leave.

"She won't go unless you come get her," Mami said to me. "Things are worsening by the day. Young people don't have a chance at life anymore," she continued. "Please get her out of here!"

As I headed to the airport, my boss called me. She was worried for my own safety as a journalist bound for Venezuela and made me promise not to go near the marches or post any pictures or information about my trip. It was torture, but I had to comply. For the first time in my career I couldn't report what I saw right away. I felt like a tourist, not a journalist.

That spring and summer, my beloved country looked like a war zone—yet again. Tear gas bombs being thrown from choppers, armed vehicles running over protesters, brutal repression in every way imaginable. Students were dying every day, and I couldn't say a word.

I remembered the old quote, "There is no agony like bearing an untold story inside you."

But I was going to fulfill my personal mission and do good by my boss. I set up camp in our childhood bedroom to help my sister pack.

"What about *abuela's* monogramed cup?" Graciela asked. "Or my college degree? I might need that."

Once again I would face the questions: *How do you fit your entire life in a suitcase? When you leave without a return ticket, what do you take with you? What do you leave behind?*

We were both privileged. We knew that. But we also knew what we were leaving—our friends, our parents, and our way of life.

As I folded Graciela's shirts, I thought about the hundreds of desperate families who come to the US border seeking a better future every year. They migrate to save their lives, full of hope and fear, knowing they do not stand a chance in their home country. Yet they also know they will not be welcomed in this new land.

Nobody goes through this unless they absolutely have to, I thought. *People don't leave everything they love unless their lives or families' lives depend on it.*

The night before Graciela and I left for the US, our parents came into the bedroom to find us sitting on the floor going through our old family albums, figuring out which ones to take. It wasn't easy. Mami had made photo albums for every year since 1984. We had spread them out on the same floor where we played with our Magic Nursery dolls and read the *Tiger Beat* magazines and comics they brought us from the US.

Now Miami, Florida, was to be our destination. It was already home base for me, but bringing Graciela over sealed the deal. We had to do it together, as we did everything in life, for the change to be definite.

"*Hijas*, remember *los valores*, the values we've taught you. Treat everyone as you would like to be treated," Mami said.

"Remember to take care of each other," Papi added.

We all hugged.

Mami then slipped a pastel blue postcard with a quote written in big white letters into my handbag. It read, "I look at them and see two sisters connected by more than blood and shared existence. Two sisters who will draw strength and encouragement from each other as they go through life. I look at them and see two sisters, two lovely daughters, and wonder . . . what have I unleashed upon the world?"

Miami, 2017

Graciela and I arrived in Florida and put our all into formulating a plan. We were incredibly lucky to have come to the United States on an airplane instead of walking through the desert or swimming in open waters risking death. Not everyone has the luxury of time and resources.

My sister came on a tourist visa. Once we arrived, we started figuring out a way to keep her in the US legally. She moved in with me in Miami, where we first inquired about seeking asylum based on the humanitarian crisis in Venezuela.

I reached out to every contact imaginable. We organized all her paperwork and went to the office of our congresswoman, Republican Ileana Ros-Lehtinen, in South Florida. (She retired in 2018.)

After a short wait, a congressional aid revealed a big folder with all the case numbers, and told us US Customs and Immigration Services were still reviewing 2013 cases.

Two thousand and thirteen! The backlog was enormous.

What was she going to do for the next five years?

The best suggestion was to secure a visa as an international student. We rounded up our savings and went to the admissions office at the University of Miami. We begged the dean to consider her application. She had good grades and strong English skills, but the deadline was two days away. After frantically pulling her application together, Graciela was accepted and enrolled in a Master's in Business Administration program.

The prospect of a graduate degree presented her with a chance to start over with an academic platform that would give her the tools she needed to develop her new passion for nonprofit work—a fresh start after the accident and a legal way to stay.

As our parents had reminded us so many times before, "Nobody can take away your education."

Again, we were lucky. Unlike many parents taking their kids across the border, we had the means to pay for an education and a pathway to safety.

While covering the mothers who brought their children across the border, I heard the same agony in their voices that I heard in my mom's first phone call: the desperation of a parent who wants their kids to have a chance at a better life.

The main difference is that these moms come here on foot, with all the burden implicit in that simple act. It's as if being poor and having been born in a country facing extreme violence or systemic poverty places them in a never-ending cycle they can't escape.

For me, their stories hit home. After all, millions of Venezuelans also fled horrific tales of abuse, prostitution, violence, corruption, and famine. Everyone I knew had a family member or spouse who was leaving—doctors, lawyers, and dentists starting over in other countries as delivery workers, Uber drivers, and valet parking employees. I saw social media videos of Venezuelan girls selling their bodies in Cúcuta on the Colombian border so they could eat. Many activists or everyday people who stayed and didn't comply with the government were imprisoned.

Weeks after Graciela and I arrived in Miami, the violence in Venezuela hit even closer to home.

I woke up trying to stop the nightmares and stories that flooded my mind. It felt awful, but I was determined to get some work done or I'd go crazy. I had a photo session for a magazine, and I wanted to try to at least *look* composed while the photographer took some shots. So I put my phone on silent for a couple of hours.

When I finally picked it up, I realized it had been going off for a while; the screen was filled with missed calls and texts.

And a name kept popping up: Reinaldo Herrera. My high school sweetheart, the boy I kissed for the first time on that starry night by the lighthouse at the beach club.

I hadn't seen him in a decade, but I knew from Instagram and our childhood friends that he was happily married and had two beautiful little girls.

I read the words but my brain refused to register them: *Fashion Designer Carolina Herrera's nephew, Reinaldo . . . Brutally Murdered in Venezuela.*

My first love, a victim to the violence I had failed to cover during my visit. He was only thirty-four years old.

His killers had tortured him so much that his face was unrecognizable. The authorities had to use forensic testing to identify him. I felt sick. On top of everything, these murky and gruesome circumstances associated him—a man I knew as noble and kind—with shady business partners and settling scores.

I was devastated. People were texting me, wanting to know gory details. I felt like screaming at the top of my lungs for them to stop. I just needed to reconnect with him in some way, to mourn him. To remember what he had taught me.

For an entire day I sat on the floor of our apartment obsessively looking for old photos of us at fifteen, sixteen, and seventeen. The innocence and hope in our smiles undid me. We had our whole lives ahead of us. Then I cried over not knowing him more, later, as an adult, as the man he became.

After our high school breakup, we grew apart. I regretted not cultivating a friendship with someone I'd shared so much with. Not reaching out. Not meeting his wife or his girls. I regretted all the things I missed and all the things I didn't say.

I was overcome with the sense that my generation was in peril.

I tried to call his mom, who was so distraught she couldn't speak. Rey's older sister, Corina, replied to me. "You of all people know he was a man of values, beloved by so many, respectful, gentlemanly, and good . . . ," she said. "With this tragedy, our family has become one more statistic of this regime, in which one of my brothers has left the country and the other fell prey to violence."

What could I do to honor his memory?

I found no other way but to put that pain into my work. I helped NBC News write the article about his murder (there was international interest because his aunt is a famous designer), includ-ing the family's words.

Months later, I told Reinaldo's story in a TEDx Talk, "Rethinking Storytelling to Help People Care."

Before a packed audience in Reno, Nevada, I spoke about his smile, his noble heart, and the injustice behind his last breath.

After I sent her the link to the talk, I heard back from his mom. "Thank you for honoring Rey's memory," she said. She asked if I had found any mementos of her son.

I gave Rey's mom the photo album I had found documenting the years of our relationship. Movie stubs. Handwritten love letters. Photos of the young boy who first taught me about love.

"*Gracias* from the bottom of my heart," she replied. "That's how I want to remember him."

Another mother dealing with separation, but this time a final one.

Whatever happened next, I resolved that in Rey's memory, I was going to try my best to make people care about any given situation I had to report. I would care about every story as if it were my own. And I would use every tool at my disposal to shed a light in dark places.

US-Mexico Border, 2018

"*Mamiiiii* . . ."

She had a face you may not recognize, but hers was a voice you can't forget.

The wailing of a little girl from Central America torn apart from her mother at the border and held inside a US government facility reverberated across the country and the world.

"Can I at least go with my aunt? I want her to come."

The wailing continued.

Her name was Alison Valencia Madrid, a six-year-old child from El Salvador recorded crying as she recited her auntie's phone number from memory.

She was being held against her will, along with ten other children.

"Mamiiii . . . Papiiii . . ." The howling was excruciating.

ProPublica published the recorded audio of the crying separated children on June 18, 2018, in which you can also hear the baffling response from a border patrol agent: "We have an orchestra here" and, "What's missing here is a conductor."

Salvadorian consulate members were able to locate Alison's aunt, who corroborated the child's identity. Photos of Alison and her mom circulated in the news, making the Trump administration's family separation policy real for so many Americans.

Alison's cry for help put a face to the crisis. It made people care.

About a month and a half before, the new so-called "Zero Tolerance" Policy had been announced by Trump's attorney general at the time, Jeff Sessions, in May 2018. He said parents crossing the border unauthorized would be referred for prosecution. This meant that parents would be placed in jail and separated from their children. The goal was to deter immigrants from coming to the southern border to seek refuge.

"If you don't like that, don't smuggle your children across our border," Sessions said during a press conference.

Approximately 2,700 kids were separated from their parents in a month and a half; 101 of these children were under five years old, according to Trump administration documents obtained by NBC News.

Our NBC News team went down to the border to give those children a voice. It was June 2018, almost two years after I'd first seen the fear in Angelina's eyes when Donald Trump won the US presidency.

This time around, inside a federal courtroom in McAllen, Texas, I saw hundreds of immigrant parents brought in shackles after their children had been taken from them. Most were "first-time offenders" from Central America.

They told the judge they were fleeing for their lives. The judge spent about a minute and a half on each case. Ninety seconds— that's all it took for their entire lives to be decided for them.

"It's like the US government is kidnapping your kid," a father named Ramón told me.

We couldn't record anything because no cameras were allowed in court. I just stood there in the back of the room, looking at their eyes and gestures. Their fear, confusion, and desperation were evident. Many were still wearing the same clothes they crossed the border in. I could see their unwashed hair, the dirt on their shoulders, no shoelaces in their shoes. Every time one of them closed their eyes or slouched the tiniest bit, the court security guard would poke them from behind.

But the worst was the sadness in their eyes; most had recently had their kids taken from them, ripped from their arms.

As an immigrant, I saw how this dehumanized all of us.

The effect on the kids was even more disheartening.

Across the street in McAllen, at a local Catholic Charities shelter run by Sister Norma Pimentel—an immigration angel who has made it her life's mission to help these families—hundreds of kids and their parents poured in. They had been detained for crossing the border and separated for short periods of time. Released and reunited, they were going to Sister Norma's for a plate of hot food, toiletries, and help getting on buses that would take them wherever they were headed, either to meet up with family or a temporary job, before appearing in immigration court.

I sat down with Cristina, a mom from El Salvador, and her two children, Robert, ten, and Aracely, sixteen, for MSNBC, translating live from Spanish to English.

"You think that it's over when you get here," Cristina said, referencing the trauma they were fleeing from in Central America, "but once you are detained here, the most painful part of the journey begins. . . . They took my young son . . . they put him in a jail cell . . . ," she added.

Robert, the ten-year-old, continued. "I asked the guard '*por qué*'—'why.' 'When will I see my mom again?' There was no answer."

He confessed on MSNBC how gangs in his native country had been trying to recruit him in school, threatening to kill his mom and sister if he didn't comply.

At ten years old and even younger, these kids are put in impossible situations. Wouldn't you be desperate to come to the United States to save your family?

Tani, a six-year-old boy, described the conditions inside the government facilities. "It was very cold. There was wire . . . I was sleeping on the floor on a tinfoil blanket. We cried the whole time there . . ."

Rooms so cold migrants called them "*la hielera,*" or "the freezer." Metal cages referred to as "*la perrera,*" or "the dog pound."

What made the isolation worse is that some of these children didn't even speak Spanish; they spoke indigenous languages derived from the Mayans like Quechua and Mam.

Story after story revealed the long-term trauma of these separations. Some children faced abuse, bullying, and the fear of not knowing anything about their parents' fate. When asked to describe what happened, many of the kids choked up to the point that my cameraman, Joe Vasquez, asked me to temporarily halt the interviews.

While the parents were being prosecuted in the courthouse at the border, the kids were scattered in facilities as far as Los Angeles, New York, and Florida.

And more were coming.

A week later we crossed the border to Reynosa, Mexico, to see if the child separation policy was actually a deterrent for migrant families.

It wasn't.

In one shelter, at least half a dozen kids and their parents were waiting to cross to the US. They had traveled for more than a month to get there, and many had been beaten, extorted, and even raped by smugglers along the way. But they explained the violence in Central America—namely Honduras, Guatemala, and El Salvador—was so bad, they had no choice.

"Gangs told us we had eighteen hours to leave the country," six-year-old Jairo told me matter-of-factly while waiting to cross the border from Mexico. "If it weren't for them, we wouldn't be here," he added, later confessing gangs had set his backpack on fire and killed his uncle in front of him.

I have been to the Syrian border and spoken to children fleeing war in the Middle East. This felt the same.

This time I set out to show all sides of the story while embedded, like a fly on the wall, with the border patrol in Laredo, Texas. I wanted to see what they were dealing with almost a month after the child separation policy was announced. Many of the agents were distraught.

"We are fathers and brothers and human beings too," Agent Gabriel Acosta said to me. He explained they saw the smugglers and cartels, who charge migrants from Central America an average of ten thousand dollars to be taken across the border, as the real enemies.

"These children are seen as commodities, left to die in the desert," Acosta added on NBC Nightly News. "And it's the only commodity we send back across the border to be extorted again and again."

What's worse is that if these traffickers get caught, the penalties are nearly nothing compared to the punishment they'd receive for smuggling drugs. As a result, many prefer to smuggle people. It's a booming industry.

Something had to give.

"Where are the children?! Where are the toddlers?!" protesters chanted outside an old warehouse turned processing center in

McAllen almost a month after we reached the border, days after the devastating ProPublica audio was released.

Rallies condemning the policy popped up all over. We set out to cover them across the country.

This crisis went beyond the Latino community.

I had never received so much support from people of all ages and backgrounds for covering a story. African Americans, Asian Americans, white Americans came up to me and thanked me for our reporting and chanted, "Where are the children?" and, "Don't criminalize immigrants!"

I even heard, "OMG! It's Mariana from TV with her hoop earrings and her heart and cross necklaces!" A dozen middle-aged white women asked me for a selfie as they started gathering for the massive "Keep Families Together" rally in Los Angeles on June 30.

Many of them had also walked in the Women's March at the beginning of the year but hadn't really come out in protest for an issue like immigration until now. "I think he's cruel, putting kids in cages. We can't stand for that," one told me, referring to President Trump.

I also saw many families, like Chris Martinez and her husband—both of whom are first-generation Mexican Americans—who marched with their two-year-old, Olivia.

Fighting back tears, Chris said to me, "I'm here because I am a mother and it breaks my heart that some moms are getting their kids taken away for no reason."

To see children, babies as young as two months old, torn away from their parents—just because they dared to come and seek asylum as refugees, fleeing from harsh conditions in their countries—that was a reality no one in this country was prepared for. Not even some people who supported President Trump and consider themselves immigration hardliners.

The public uproar was too much for the administration. On June 20, 2018, Trump reversed course and signed an executive order officially overturning the family separation policy, although some parents and children are still being affected and have yet to be reunited as of mid 2019.

The media had shed light on a story that otherwise wouldn't have gotten much attention because it was about undocumented children. It was one of those rare instances when you immediately see the fruits of your work as a journalist and the power of giving people a voice.

But our reporting was needed more than ever. Pulling the families apart was easy. Putting them back together proved more challenging.

The NBC team and I, including persistent reporters like Jacob Soboroff, were at the border for months. There were reports of children returned covered with lice. Children who hadn't been bathed. And children who had allegedly been physically and sexually abused, whose traumatized parents said their personalities had completely changed.

Across the country, from one airport to the next, from Chicago to Los Angeles, all the way down to Florida and Houston, I witnessed reunifications where the kids shied away from their parents. Disoriented. Vacant. The sense of abandonment had broken their spirits.

One mom, Raquel, was separated from her two sons, Christopher, thirteen, and Yeremi, nine. Yeremi is on the autism spectrum and was held in a different facility than his older brother. She explained the process to me on the air for MSNBC. "Every week they'd ask, 'When are you coming to get us?' 'Why don't you try harder, Mom? You don't love us anymore.'"

After three months of separation, Raquel was reunited with her two boys and is living with her parents in Los Angeles. Her first court date for asylum was in early 2019.

Inside the Port Isabel detention facility this past July, where separated parents remain incarcerated, Santos Sacul Choco, a thirty-two-year-old mother from Guatemala separated from her fourteen-year-old son, Carlos Enrique, looked at me in despair through a thick glass window.

She clung to the black prison-like phone and told me, "Don't forget us."

She represents hundreds. I am including her story here so we don't.

During one of the final weeks of our coverage that July, I was able to talk to Alison, the six-year-old Salvadorian girl whose leaked audio helped turned the tide on the border crisis, and her mom, Cindi Madrid, just hours after their reunification.

I asked Alison what her message was to those kids still separated. "Keep fighting and be strong, because soon you will be with your parents," she said, holding on to a doll. "Have faith."

After everything that happened to her, this little girl had

enough spirit to encourage others. It was the same faith that made her speak up and recite her aunt's phone number, changing the course of events.

I couldn't help but think how millions from my own home country, including me and my sister, had started fleeing by plane, by boat, and even on foot the previous year.

In all these cases, the only choice had been to act—to do something, anything, to get to safety. *Nobody goes through this unless they absolutely have to*, I'd thought at the time. The memories felt painfully fresh.

Former president Ronald Reagan often called the United States "a shining city upon a hill." That's a statement of leadership and hope, especially to us immigrants born on the other side of the hill.

The shining lights of this city give us hope that democracy, a better today, a better tomorrow, are possible. No matter how bad things get, one can still see the light—through the eyes of the children. As we battle through this crisis, sometimes it feels that all we can do is take little Alison's words to heart—keep fighting and be strong. Have faith.

#*Go like Mariana*: Sometimes we can forget that the headlines in the news are about real people. Let's remember: it could happen to any of us. How would *you* want to be treated?

11

A Million Likes for You

Washington, DC, March 2018

I never really considered myself an "influencer," even though some of my colleagues refer to me as one. What I can tell you is how the stories I've encountered have fueled me, how they have made me passionate about communicating and helping people in new ways. This passion and commitment span both traditional and social media, are reflected in two languages, and feel deeply rooted in my own story.

"*Hola, mi gente!*" I say every morning to the almost half a million people on my social media platforms as Peter Shaw—my usually disapproving, old-school-at-heart producer—pouts at me (he finally got that *mi gente* means "my people," and it's pronounced *hen-tay*). I pretend not to notice and keep posting. "We are covering the March for Our Lives protest against gun violence. Let me know if and why you are marching today."

That particular day was a cold Saturday in March, and thousands of high schoolers and their families were protesting in Washington, DC, demanding gun reform after the February 2018 deadly school shooting in Parkland, Florida, that killed seventeen students.

Thirty minutes after I posted my videos on social media, I started getting thousands of likes, comments, and direct messages from people all around the country and the world. I relished the immediacy and the interaction.

Besides my traditional news platform, social media is a way to bring people additional information and engage with them directly. Sometimes people online will alert me to things I didn't know about a local story or angles I hadn't considered about a national debate.

Every good old-school reporter will tell you that the best thing to do when you parachute in to cover a story in a new place is to talk to taxi drivers, people in local restaurants, and business owners, because they will always share good tips. For me, interacting with *mi gente*, my community of followers, is the same—just with a digital spin.

Most importantly, it's the way to reach audiences who aren't going to see me on the six o'clock news or on cable. My Instagram and Facebook feeds provide an unfiltered look behind the scenes of the news. I'm not duplicating information but constantly adding value. It's like lifting the curtain, which allows me to be more informal and real. That rawness has spilled over to TV.

Instead of standing in front of the Capitol building for live shots of the protests, Peter and I suggested being live on MSNBC from inside a van with a group of students who had made their way from Kentucky to the rally in DC.

As I'm sitting in the back of the van, the smells of puberty and Cheetos hit me. Instantly, I'm back in Venezuela, remembering our protests, our youth and energy (and junk-food addiction). It's admirable how fierce and committed young people can be when they rally behind a cause.

We found the teens and their chaperones on social media after reading a local Kentucky article. Otherwise, finding a group of forty kids making their way across the country would have been like finding a needle in a haystack.

Social media is one of the best tools for news gathering; it helps us locate ideas, inspiration, and characters for stories. But it also lets people know what you are up to. There is no one too big or too small for this wave. As individuals organize and personalize their platforms, it's becoming clear that this is a phenomenon that encompasses everyone.

While we broadcasted on cable and I went live on my feeds, the students themselves were live on their own social media platforms, creating a ripple effect of direct coverage you can't get through traditional media. They added our stories to their own feeds and even told their friends to watch the coverage on TV.

This generation gets it. The Parkland kids were able to gain national attention and organize thanks to social media. After the shooting, Emma Gonzalez, one of the leading faces from Marjory Stoneman Douglas High School in Florida, amassed almost a million Twitter followers in a week.

Once we reached the Capitol, the students joined countless other gun-reform activists.

I spoke to Nicole Hockley, a mom who lost her six-year-old son, Dylan, in the tragic shooting at Sandy Hook Elementary in Newtown, Connecticut, where twenty-year-old Adam Lanza killed twenty schoolchildren and six teachers in 2012. The parents had since formed a group called Sandy Hook Promise, currently directed by Nicole. Through their organization, they've provided programs, training, and advocacy for more than 5.5 million parents, students, and community leaders.

"If we had social media back then, we would have had a better chance at getting Congress to act," she said.

Parkland was the deadliest school shooting since Sandy Hook, but only six years later things have totally changed—in large part due to social media. Big networks don't own the sole communication channels. Facebook, Twitter, Instagram, Snapchat, and so many other platforms have become game changers.

In such a sea of voices, how do you find your own? How do you stand out? How do you help people? It's about being real.

Even though I mostly stream or post in English, my "*Hola, mi gente*" greeting in Spanish and my use of Spanglish are true to who I am and my background. The audience's response to authenticity is always immediate.

"Thank you so much for doing this. Now I know I can do this and not be judged or taken less seriously," one Latinx follower posted.

While I've often been frustrated with traditional media for not allowing for much range, social media lets you show all your sides, your fears, and your imperfections. The truth is, we are all brilliantly flawed. You don't have to be perfect—just perfectly you.

By being real we are helping to push boundaries of what's acceptable, especially for young people.

"*Hola, mi gente,*" which might have thrown off some of my English-speaking colleagues in the beginning, has now become so well liked that I closed the on-air NBC campaign for Hispanic Heritage Month with the phrase. Then I added a "*Pa'lante*"—"Let's go!"

Social media is not a nine-to-five job. It can be an extension of the self—a form of self-expression. And it's so much better if we can stay real in our posts. What would I gain by pretending to do cooking tips if I can barely cook? Putting out a fake version of myself based on what's popular would only backfire, because your social media will follow you forever.

Case in point: I did one makeup tutorial because it's what many bloggers do and it's extremely click friendly. But I'm not really into that. I do basic makeup and am out the door for my reporting in five minutes.

Still, I recorded the video in my bathroom showing the camera all the products I use for a "smoky eye," which looked so forced. I ended up deleting it after a while. It wasn't me. Can you imagine if it had gone viral? I would have felt pressure to continue doing something that didn't feel natural.

It's so much better to put your real self out there.

———

But here's the caveat. That lesson we all learned in high school is still true: being out there also makes you vulnerable—and an easier target.

Houston, 2017

I was standing in the rain outside Houston Methodist Hospital in Texas, covering one of late president George H.W. Bush's many hospitalizations when I got a text from a friend.

"Are you sitting down?" she wrote.

Nothing good usually comes after this, I thought. I waited until I was off the air to respond.

It was my friend Verónica Ruiz del Vizo, one of the most creative and kindest human beings on the planet. She's also my social media guru (an integral part of my squad of good people).

"Someone just published a horrible article about you," she said.

"MSNBC's Mariana Atencio: Rich, Gorgeous, Famous and a Victim," the headline read.

I felt a punch in the gut. Big exhale. Count to one hundred. I did need to sit down for this one.

The lengthy article on a conservative blog went on to criticize everything I did, from my social media posts about the Hispanic community—calling me a Latina chauvinist—to what it referred to as the "left leaning" editorial at MSNBC and Univision, and even my husband and grandparents. I couldn't help but take it to heart. They were demoralizing both my work and my family.

One of the author's main criticisms was of my looks. Calling me a fair-skinned Latina and asking why I don't look like many of the "illegal immigrants flooding over America's southern border." (Again, really? It gets old telling people that Latinos come in all shapes, sizes, and ethnic types.)

Still, my first reaction was asking, "How did I offend this person? What did I do wrong?"

"That's exactly how a woman would react," Verónica said to me. "Instead of brushing it off or shutting it down, you are worried about how the color of *your skin* and *your background*—things you have absolutely no control over—offended a man who doesn't know you."

Women have this worry a lot when they are criticized: *What did I do to elicit this?*

"This author never would have written *this* about another man, you know." Verónica hit the nail on the head.

"You need to stay true to yourself on social media and on TV, not only for you, but for the many young women out there who will also be attacked like this," she concluded.

Even though I tried to disregard the criticism and haven't written about it until now, she was right. Isn't it funny how the inevitable "haters" can help us grow?

Just as a friend convinces you to listen to a new song or to travel to their favorite city, Verónica introduced me to the power of social media.

A single mom, struggling to make it in Venezuela after her own mother tragically passed away when she was only seventeen, Verónica was an unlikely person to have founded a social media empire.

But she did it.

She had a little music magazine that started promoting its content on Facebook in 2004—the first year of the social media company—and she did it so well that Pepsi took notice and bought online ad space as a way of reaching those cool musician kids in South America.

Verónica saw an opportunity and turned that magazine into a startup, Mashup Interactive Agency. Eleven years later she represents 45 top multinational brands on social media, manages 115 employees, and has offices in places like New York, Miami, Colombia, and Panama. All while being an amazing mother to her now ten-year-old daughter, Charlotte.

Every time I'm about to launch something big on social media, Verónica reminds me of these important points:

- What is your goal?
- Who is your audience?
- What's missing? Look at what your competitors are doing; don't copy them but fill in the blanks.
- Content is king. Flimsy photos with no substance won't get you far.
- Engage with your community.
- But also adjust. Not even Lele Pons gets it right the first time around. It's trial and error, a conversation—or, as I find time and time again, a sociological experiment.

As a person who has never had access to a traditional media outlet, she's taught me to think of a social media component to everything I do, especially when there are opportunities for helping and empowering others.

When students from the University of Reno in Nevada picked me to give my first TEDx Talk, they wanted to hear from more diverse speakers. When I found out the tickets cost around one hundred dollars, I called Verónica.

"It doesn't seem fair," I told her. "These kids wanted to hear from me, and it's going to be challenging for them to attend."

"Why don't you get the TEDx folks to give away some tickets on your behalf when people engage with the event and content on social?" she suggested. "It's a win-win for everyone."

The title of my talk was "What Makes You Special?" And since my message focused on embracing our differences, we launched a viral campaign urging people to celebrate what makes them unique. They had to post a photo of themselves making the peace sign and using the hashtags #Humanist, #TedxUNR, and, of course, #GoLikeMariana.

The response was overwhelming. The TEDx folks then selected five winners to be my personal guests.

I have to say, getting off that stage in front of more than a thousand people to hug new friends who had made it all the way to Reno because of this social media contest we came up with made the experience so much more enriching.

In fact, the organizers turned "What Makes You Special?" into the theme of the whole 2017 conference. Everyone got a name tag at the front door with blank spaces that read:

My name is _____.

What makes me special is _____.

Looking at people's comments and reactions—celebrating their uniqueness, opening up about how they felt judged by their looks, talking about how they overcame stereotypes and stuck to being themselves—was the best way to recover from that negative article.

As of this writing, my TEDx Talk, "What Makes You Special?" has more than eight million views and has been translated into eight languages.

Every week I get an avalanche of texts, emails, and direct messages from people all over the world—like Patrick Mugabo from Rwanda's Kigali, Dana Marie from San Diego, Ma Soudou from Morocco, Eddie Sandoval from Wichita, and eleven-year-old Sophia Yun from Korea—telling me how they have also felt different at times, but my story and message has helped them realize it isn't something to be ashamed of but rather celebrated.

Here is Sophia's email.

Dear Role Model:

Hello! I really hope you read this email, but I know it has a small chance.

I am an eleven-year-old girl all the way from Korea.

You are my role model!

My friends have role models that are famous celebrities and presidents, but mine is specifically you and some other people.

I watched your TED talk, "What makes you special?" about a few months ago.

I simply loved it! So I shared it with my family and they liked it too.

I could agree with the things you say about my experience, I moved schools to an international school at Thailand when I never even met foreigners.

Now I learned a lot from my experience and myself, I am an international at Korea.

I love watching TED talks. It's how I find a lot to learn and how I enjoy my own time.

I think "When you're different, you have to work at belonging" is the most touching thing you said in the video.

I love your lesson and I am sure you changed a lot of people's perspective in this world.

Well, I just wanted to let you know, that you are a role model to one eleven-year-old girl all the way across the sea.

I watched your videos over 4 times and I will watch it again some days.

Thank you so much for speaking such a beautiful speech and shaking up the world peacefully.

You are amazing, thank you more if you read this and I am so happy.

> Sincerely, Sophia K.
> —Friends can change your life when
> you are enough to change theirs—
> Sophia Kwon Class of 2024

No doubt the social media campaign helped this message spread its wings all the way across the sea. Not because we forced it to, but because the content was genuine. It all came naturally. By being ourselves, we can connect with people who truly find value in our identity. It's so much better than chasing after viral status.

This brings me to my last point, and probably the most important: How do you go beyond the coveted million likes and actually *help* people using social media?

The potential is infinite. Going about it is different from establishing a presence online, but the main questions are the same: What is your goal? How do you want to help your audience? What's missing out there?

I was getting ready to host the Bronx Museum of Arts Gala in New York when Verónica called me with a concern in mind.

"I see so much happening around the #MeToo movement and women needing to be empowered around the world," she said. "Let's do something about it."

"Sign me up," I replied without skipping a beat.

Next thing I knew, Verónica and our friend Maickel Melamed—a business coach, motivational speaker, and high-performance athlete with special needs—rounded up a group of influencers and experts on different topics (a psychologist, a blogger mom, a marketing pro, an actress, yours truly, etc.) to help. The idea was to launch an e-learning website where we all share knowledge and experiences through taped e-courses, many downloadable for free. We discussed how to deal with sexual harassment (Verónica herself confessed to being a victim) and how to empower women in all corners of the world. We would spread the word and provide the content using social media.

That same month, on International Women's Day, DAR Learning was born.

Dar means "giving" in Spanish, so we call ourselves "givers." Twenty influencers and experts from places like Mexico, Venezuela, and Colombia offer courses like "How Much Is Your Talent Worth?," "5 Basic Principles to Be an Entrepreneur," "Techniques for Public Speaking," and my e-class, "How to Be a Wonder Woman in Media."

In less than a year, we've provided fifteen hundred scholarships (free access to the whole site and courses for a year) to women all over the world. Our goal is to give six thousand scholarships a year. Seven thousand people apply on average every month, and we've gotten applications from places as far and wide as Ecuador, Italy, Germany, and Canada.

The World Economic Forum and the American Embassy in Venezuela have told Verónica they are interested in financing the platform, so the operating costs will go down. It's a direct way of helping people wherever they are—without needing a huge investment— thanks to social media. The possibilities are truly endless.

I was thinking about the power of a Twitter feed as the sun beamed on that cold day in Washington during the March for Our Lives protest in spring 2018. It felt as if that moment would mark a generation. Energetic. Busy. Historic.

At least half a million young people and their families were holding banners and phones. Most of the signs had some sort of message about change.

The revolution is here, and it has nothing to do with party politics. It is all about the future.

That national student rally—one of the biggest since Vietnam—showcased diversity on stage, but also in the crowds. We heard from people of every ethnicity—kids who didn't let gender or age define them, breaking stereotypes to create the America most people want to see.

With social media, we have a power that no other generation has had before. To unite, push the world forward, and see the amazing results.

It's not about a million likes, and it's not what you look like or what you do; it's about who you are and what you stand for.

#*Go like Mariana*: In life and online, the truth is, we are all brilliantly flawed. You don't have to be perfect—just perfectly you.

12

Losing My Dad and My Country

Caracas, February 2018

This can't be happening, I said to myself.

Driving around in the city I used to call home, I closed my eyes again and again, hoping to find the views that my memory kept conjuring. It was a useless exercise. The magic was gone.

The streets of Caracas, where I learned to ride a bike, grabbed lunch at my dad's *arepera,* and protested against the increasingly authoritarian government during college, were now abandoned and crumbling in every sense—with corruption, violence, and decaying buildings.

During months of protests over the spring and summer, only seven months earlier, dozens of students had been killed, and I had been forced to take my sister to the United States. Now the streets were practically empty. The young protesters fled for their lives, too, when the protests waned in the fall of 2017.

I was back because my dad got the flu that was going around in the United States. As much as I saw him as my timeless hero, he was seventy-two years old, and that year the strain of the flu was proving deadly for many people his age, as well as young children under the age of five.

It all happened so fast. Dad started feeling under the weather in Venezuela after spending the holidays in Florida with us. Because he didn't live in the US, he didn't see the need to get the flu shot. Even though there are many other diseases in Venezuela, the yearly strain of the flu isn't an issue because of the tropical weather.

My brother called on a Tuesday morning while I was on a shoot for TV.

"Papi has been taken to the ICU with complex pneumonia caused by the flu," he began. "The doctors say he can die," he added stiffly.

This time I didn't freeze the way I had when I learned about Graciela's accident. I didn't lose sense of where I was. I was keenly aware of my surroundings and the urgency of making a plan with my family.

"The doctors don't have anything to treat him," Alvaro Elias continued. "And he's too fragile to be moved to the States. Please come as soon as possible with whatever meds are required."

"What's wrong?" Peter, my producer, asked when I hung up the phone. I probably looked like I'd seen a ghost. "We need to mic you to start," he said.

I was in a coffee shop in Pittsburgh about to do a panel on Millennials running for office. I had four young mayors from the area, a crew of about eight people, four cameras, and dozens of lights, all watching me and waiting for me to begin.

"I need a minute," I uttered as I walked to the restroom hallway and started to count.

By the time I got to twenty I had managed to calm down.

I had read the headlines on the health crisis in my home country, but living through it firsthand would prove a daily struggle for my father's survival unlike anything I'd experienced.

I needed to be there for my father, to be the rock he would have been for me.

Glancing down at my watch, I realized it was 8:45 a.m—right before the daily editorial conference call. I had just enough time to call my boss and explain what was happening.

My voice trembled, but I didn't cry.

"Leave as soon as possible," she said without hesitation. "Family always comes first."

The unconditional support provided by my managers and colleagues would mean everything to me in the month ahead.

Meanwhile, over the next few hours, my family made crucial decisions. My brother and I would go to Venezuela to help Mami, while my husband and sister—who had just started her studies and could lose her immigration status if she left the US—would stay in Miami to procure whatever meds my father needed, given the shortages in Venezuela. Our plan was to send the extra supplies with whoever was traveling down there each day, either close friends or acquaintances.

Back in Pittsburgh, Peter, who by then had become like another sibling to me, helped me look for flights. I still needed to fly back to Miami first with enough time to find Dad's medicine, and the next direct flight to Venezuela from Miami wouldn't leave for another full day.

While my brother texted me the initial list of pills, vials, and antibiotics, I mustered the courage to host the panel. I felt that this was the moment to prove how professional and strong I had become. The young politicians being interviewed had no idea that anything was wrong, but months later, in coordination with Peter, all the interviewees graciously sent me a signed greeting card with a prayer.

After a two-day frantic search in pharmacies and medical supply stores all over South Florida and a mad dash to the airport, I arrived at Simon Bolivar International Airport in Venezuela with $5,000 worth of medicine, all used to beat flu-related infections, in my bags: Trimethoprim (800 mg)—96 doses in injectable form; Voriconazole (200 mg)—20 doses in injectable form; and fifteen pills of Prednisone (50 mg).

"How are we going to solve this, Ms. Atencio?" the customs agent asked as she stared at the contents of my suitcase in the "socialist control" backroom. Not everyone gets flagged at customs down there, but they probably spotted the carry-on stuffed with medicine in the TSA machine. Unlike the US, in Venezuela you have to screen your bags when you enter the country. Since there are massive shortages of everything and the socialist military controls the airport, you're pretty much at the mercy of whoever is doing security that day.

I noticed the guard's eyes eagerly looking at a stick of butter in my handbag. (Yes, *butter*! The one thing my aunt asked me to bring for her.) Like other basic goods, butter had also become so rare in Venezuela it was the equivalent of liquid gold.

I turned over the butter and a couple of hundred dollars in taxes to get by customs. Not a bad start. Not exactly ethical, but it was also a matter of life or death.

My taxi driver from the airport was a former gym teacher. He said teaching didn't pay much, so he earned four times more driving people around. And even then, cash was scarce.

Papi was hospitalized at Centro Médico, or Medical Center of Caracas, one of the most prestigious private clinics in the country, where top-notch doctors find themselves desperate for basic drugs to do their jobs. The local pharmaceutical association estimates there is a shortage of 85 percent of drugs in Venezuela.

"He hasn't gotten worse," his infectologist told me when I arrived, "but there's a problem." My stomach tightened.

"Clarithromycin, one of the antibiotics he was responding to, ran out. You need to find it for us."

"Why didn't you tell me before?" I replied, visibly irritated. After all, I had gotten everything on their list.

"I'm not a pharmacist," she stated matter-of-factly. "We thought the hospital had enough, but our stock suddenly depleted."

I grabbed my phone in a rush and put out the information via text message, WhatsApp chats, and social media. Hundreds of people immediately offered to help. Some were acquaintances; others were complete strangers who might have the medicine at home. If I thought I'd witnessed the power of social media before, this showed me its positive power on a whole new level.

After months of shortages, everyone in Venezuela understands what need is. They feel isolated from the rest of the world, so they bond in a wave of solidarity. They know that any day, the person in need could be them or someone they love.

Other friends of friends and even *vecinos*, neighbors, put me in touch with people who operate in the black market for medicine. They are called *bachaqueros*, or "red ants." These "ants" trade any known supply—including blood (blood banks are depleted too)—and can also quickly bring meds from abroad. Just like those selling black market goods in most dystopian thrillers, they have aliases, and their responses include strict instructions for wire transfers and door-to-door deliveries via motorcycles.

Three weeks into his illness, Papi's kidneys started failing. We were told he would need dialysis treatment and were presented with the biggest challenge yet.

"We have the dialysis machine, but not the actual bags with the fluid," Dr. Jerry Gomez, who was in charge of the ICU, told me. "You need to find forty bags of five liters each for him to complete the treatment."

We shared the message with all our contacts and quickly realized the only way to get ahold of and mobilize such a large quantity of dialysis fluid bags—and fast enough—would be finding it in neighboring Colombia and smuggling it across the border.

We got the name of the manufacturer, and relatives in Colombia set out to contact them.

Unfortunately, the manufacturer wouldn't sell to patients in Venezuela because of US sanctions against the Maduro government. But a friend found a doctor willing to create a fake patient's case in order to get the company to sell the bags.

Now we just had to figure out how to bring the forty bags from Colombia to Venezuela.

My brother got off the phone with a smile. "Our uncle has a friend who used to import books from Colombia. He has a contact who can place the bags in his truck to carry them across the border."

As a law-abiding citizen and a journalist, I thought about the ethics behind the whole situation. In the past weeks, I had come into the country with an undisclosed number of antibiotics, texted with black market traders who were partly to blame for hoarding meds and hiking up prices, forged a patient's medical record in another country, and was arranging to smuggle dialysis fluid across the border. But with Dad's life on the line, I had no sense of what was right and wrong anymore.

A struggle for survival—that's everyday life in Venezuela for so many people, as though Venezuelans are living in some weird Latin American sequel to *The Hunger Games*.

When we told the medical staff our plan to get the dialysis bags, they seemed genuinely relieved. I later got an *"Excelente trabajo—great job!"* text from one of the doctors.

Once again, I was aware of how lucky I was. Even though my bank account and credit cards were taking a beating, at least we were able to find and pay for what we needed.

My local Twitter feed showed a protest by dialysis patients in the city of Barquisimeto, southwest of Caracas, demanding treatment and supplies. They were carrying signs that read, "We want to live" and, "Dialysis now," as President Nicolás Maduro was celebrating the triumphs of *La Revolución* on national TV.

"The best is yet to come," Maduro stated with a laugh. His government had stopped importing medicine, denied humanitarian aid from other nations, and even blocked shipments of medicine from the US.

This had to be cynicism at its best. Or maybe he had no concept of the massive health crisis happening all over a country that was once the richest in South America because it did not affect him or anyone close to him.

His response made the situation all the more incomprehensible.

Over the total course of three weeks, I spent every waking minute inside the ICU, getting to know the doctors and nurses treating my dad. Their stories were a sad reflection of the new normal there.

The brain drain was alarming. There is no next generation to change the guard.

Dr. Francisco Javier Márquez, president of the hospital, told me that 75 percent of the doctors at the Medical Center of Caracas had left over the last two years. He explained he had seen headhunters from Ecuador poaching his well-trained staff in the halls. Only

15 percent of the remaining doctors in the hospital were under the age of fifty-five.

Because Venezuela has the highest inflation in the world, domestic medical insurance policies don't hold up. Dr. Márquez told me this keeps most people from seeking medical treatment, leaving them to die and causing hospitals to close. The Medical Center of Caracas has seventy-five hospital beds, and only twenty-five have been filled on average this year.

"It's not just us; if this situation continues, all hospitals in Venezuela will have to close their doors," he confessed sadly.

Addys Gamboa, the twenty-year-old nurse who worked the afternoon shift, was leaving for Chile. "I will be able to afford to live with my salary," she said. She had a sister waiting for her there and had heard the revalidation of her nursing license would be relatively quick.

Thirty-seven-year-old Dr. Laura Sánchez, a critical care physician in the ICU, said she frequently had to treat patients who couldn't afford the procedures they needed. "Sometimes I feel irresponsible about doing my job this way, because you know the tools that should be available, especially in this globalized world, and you just don't have them," she admitted. "As doctors, our hands are tied."

But the fact that they are still there, doing their best, reveals a lot about the resilience required to stay in Venezuela.

"This is pure vocation, because everything else is working against you," said Dr. Jorge Valery, my dad's main doctor and cardiologist.

"There is a sense of mysticism and camaraderie when you work in these conditions," he added. "You have to try to save lives no matter what."

That's what they did. Every day. Regardless of the dire conditions, I saw Dr. Valery and the team at Centro Médico's ICU pour their hearts and souls into my dad's recovery.

Unlike what would have been my role in most other countries, my role here wasn't to be a bystander relegated to the hospital's waiting room. I played a key part: to obtain my father's medicine. I lived and breathed it. I had made a corner of the ICU my own. I was part of the team.

That's why it hit me twice as hard when Papi's body gave out—a day after we had finally managed to get the dialysis bags.

The landline rang in our apartment in Caracas before dawn, and my gut told me it was the end. We rushed to the hospital, and when we arrived the doctor informed us my dad had suffered from sepsis-induced cardiac arrest. Although the ICU team had resuscitated him multiple times, in the end every effort failed.

His voice trailed off.

I couldn't make out the rest of it. My mind tuned out. I just heard my mom wail as she threw herself over my father's body. It's a sound I'll never forget. A primal cry. A wounded animal's whine. She's usually so strong. My sister followed suit. My brother and I were numb.

After what seemed like an eternity, my mother, sister, and brother left the room. They couldn't stand the pain for another minute. Being his firstborn, I felt I had to stay with him for as long as I could. I stood in my corner of the ICU, tears rolling down my cheeks. I pulled up YouTube on my phone and played a song from our favorite movie, *Casablanca*'s "As Time Goes By." It was the same song I would hear coming from his green study at home some nights and the song that was playing the night I confessed I wanted to be a journalist. I listened to it on repeat until my father was placed in a black body bag.

A million images came to my mind. I remembered Papi teaching me to swim in the waters of the Caribbean during *Carnaval* holiday. His calm and deep reflections after 9/11. And that chilly October night when he walked me to the Emmy Awards and saw his little warrior princess come into her own.

"I hoped for a different ending," Dr. Jerry Gomez, the head of the ICU, told me as the coroner took my father away.

"I did too," I replied.

Not only for my dad, but also for Venezuela.

My father believed in Venezuela's recovery until his last breath. But for me, hope that my country would get better any time soon left with him.

The next morning I opened the newspaper at our breakfast table. It had been part of Papi's routine. When I saw his name in the obituary section, I was broken by the pain in those black letters. It was the saddest story, a reminder that we are all a step away from having our names printed there.

Speaking at his packed memorial service in Caracas on behalf of my family, looking over at his friends, at the doctors and nursing staff who had briefly left their posts at the ICU to be there, I pushed back tears.

How could I describe the simplicity and immensity of my dad with words? Have you ever tried embracing a sequoia tree? That's how Papi made me feel. He was, at the same time, rooted on earth but always pushing toward the sky . . . big, protective, nurturing—he gave me shade and strength. And I could easily imagine the birds that he loved so much making a nest on his infinite branches.

Staring down at his coffin, I started out by speaking the truth.

Papi, it's impossible to express how I feel.

There is no measure that can quantify what you mean to me—no song, poem, painting, or sunset that encompasses how much I love you.

Thank you a thousand times, because you didn't just give us a house; you and Mami gave us a home.

Thank you for teaching us to be real, to say what we mean—with respect, but without fear—to fight for what we want, working hard to achieve it, without envying anyone else.

Thank you for teaching us to appreciate everything in life. From art, music, culture, languages, to the fact that we were born on this land, and the importance of just saying "*Buenos días*" with a smile when we walked into an elevator.

You had the gift of alchemy: to transform the simplest things into the extraordinary.

I finished by reading a poem:

Death is nothing at all. . . .
I have only slipped away to the next room. . . .

I am I, and you are you . . .
Whatever we were to each other, that we still are.
Call me by the old familiar name.
Speak of me in the easy way which you always used. . . .
I am but waiting for you, for an interval,
somewhere very near,
just round the corner.

There was nothing more to say except that I knew Papi would live in me, always.

As I boarded my return flight to Miami, I thought about what I was leaving behind—my mom, the patients at that hospital in Caracas, the doctors, and the millions of people who can't afford basic medical care. I looked out the airplane window and clung to the little wooden box holding my dad's ashes.

So many more will die, I thought. A part of me died there too.

My world had changed forever, but routine life had to go on. I know Papi would have wanted it that way.

Two weeks later, I had to fulfill the commitment I'd made to host the Bronx Museum of the Arts Gala, an opportunity that had come through an old friend of my dad's from New York, Latin jazz musician Eddie Palmieri. The night's proceeds gave access to arts education to children from underprivileged communities.

I still had a hard time getting out of bed. I had lost weight and didn't know if I could speak in public so soon. But I wanted to help those kids.

I mustered all my strength to go back to the city we both loved so much, get on stage in a black and white gown, and say, "Papi, *esto es por ti*—this is for you!"

Walking around New York the day after, I went into St. Patrick's Cathedral. Just as I knelt before La Virgen de Guadalupe, a little red chirping bird flew into the church.

Eres tú.

I knew it was him.

Little by little I began to sense his presence in everything I did and everyone who approached me. By opening up about loss, I connected to others in a way I hadn't before.

One day my friend and one of my mentors, MSNBC anchor Ali Velshi, told me his mother-in-law was very ill. I offered my love and support. When she passed, I sent him a text with the poem I had read at my father's funeral.

"These words brought me great comfort," Ali texted back. "It means a lot, especially from someone who is still going through it. The memories will long outlive the pain . . . Thank you."

Loss changes us and our stories, and yet connects us.

A month later I penned a news story for NBCNews.com about Papi's tragic passing to shed light on the crisis in Venezuela.

Titled "In the Chaos of Venezuela, a Daughter Fights for Her Father's Life," the article was woven from my notes and recollections from my time at the hospital. It was the most painful thing I'd ever put down on paper.

The response was striking, not only from colleagues, but from folks on both sides of the aisle condemning the health crisis in Venezuela, and from hundreds on social media.

Every day people sent messages of encouragement. Some told me how they were holding on to hope for their loved ones; others talked about how they were coping with their own losses. Their openness and generosity were overwhelming.

Chandler on Instagram said:

I lost my dad to heart failure a bit ago. I know. I know. One moment. One hour. One day at a time.

Oli from New York messaged me, saying:

I know the pain you are feeling. I lost my mother in 2006 and she was only 58 years old. A mother and father's love is eternal and transcends all realms . . . Your father will always be with you. Just pay attention to the signs and you'll know.

One of Papi's signs was the opportunity to help Venezuela and its children—to remember where I came from.

For his birthday, on April 4, my sister and I collected donations and bought a thousand nutritional meal supplements to feed kids in need in our home country.

Since I knew people in Venezuela struggled with accountability and making sure the donations went to the right people, I personally distributed them at JM de Los Rios Children's Hospital in Caracas, where four hundred kids don't even get two meals a day.

We had to walk up the stairs since there was no power. Looking at their little faces light up over bottles of Ensure, I saw Papi everywhere. This was the best way to honor his memory: to keep hope alive.

The weeks following his passing were tough, healing, and hopeful all at the same time. They showed me even more how sharing our stories and what we care about can bring connection and empathy in times of chaos and tragedy. Healing can come from lifting our voices and opening our hearts.

#Go like Mariana: Loss changes us and our stories, and yet connects us. We remember the ones who teach us to be real, to say what we mean—with respect, but without fear—to fight for what we want, working hard to achieve it.

13

Shelter from the Storm

Oak Island, North Carolina, August 2018

A storm was raging. I'd been sleeping in a stranger's bunk bed for five days. We were stranded on an island with no water while covering a hurricane for NBC News.

Big networks go big on weather stories. They deploy almost all their talent wherever a Category 4 hurricane will hit or a tornado is likely to do extreme damage, which means everyone is fighting for airtime with the big dogs like Al Roker and Jim Cantore—and each team is out on their own.

For reporters, it's a race against time. You need to stock up on food and supplies before the weather comes; you cover "preps" (locals getting ready, gassing up, boarding up); you monitor the forecast to get your team situated in the weather "elements"; but you can't be too daring in picking your spot, because most of the time you need a cell signal to be live on TV. It's a tricky balance. Plus, additional hurdles arise once the natural disaster strikes: flooded roads, no gas, and no hotel rooms. This explains why I found myself waking up in a stranger's guest bed for the fifth day in a row.

The task was covering Hurricane Florence in North Carolina. We started out in Wilmington, but the eye of the storm was headed directly there, so we opted to drive forty minutes south to Oak Island, North Carolina, a strategic location to cover the beaches and storm surge. When the island's bridges closed, however, we found ourselves homeless on the night of the hurricane.

"How are you preparing, sir?" I asked a sixty-two-year-old local man, live on the air.

"Well, I am prepared to hunker down for weeks. I have a generator, a water well, and a radio transmitter," he answered.

Off-air, I jokingly asked, "Are you married? Do you have a big family? Can you take in four human rescues?"

His name was Paul Gawin. When he heard we had no place to go, he put us up for what was supposed to be a night and turned into five. Aside from making us soup, one night he sang songs from *West Side Story* because he said I reminded him of Maria. Not only did he host us, but he came *with us* to cover the storm, acting as our local guide.

Some call this Southern hospitality; I offer no explanation other than God is always with us. This man we didn't know practically saved our lives when he gave us shelter from the storm.

The rest of my crew was camped out on the sofa and guest bedroom. I heard the sound of Billie Myers's 1997 song "Kiss the Rain" go off at 4:00 a.m. It was my producer's alarm clock. Even at that hour, I couldn't help but laugh out loud. *Really, Peter, that's what you wake up to?* My tune is The Beatles' "Here Comes the Sun."

Field teams at the network level are usually made up of four people: correspondent, producer, photographer, and soundman. Although the last two change depending on the assignment, I've been working with Peter Shaw for the past year. Originally from California, he's the epitome of the all-American white guy; he has blue eyes and a football-player build. He's a hard worker and as square as they come, and whenever he has a free minute he is usually FaceTiming with his wife and one-year-old son. His grandma is none other than legendary actress Angela Lansbury.

Peter doesn't speak a lick of Spanish and rolls his eyes at most of my social media posts, cultural references, and emotional meltdowns. By his own admission, it took him a month to get my full name down to book travel arrangements for me, spelling out: "Mariana del Carmen Atencio Cervoni." We fight like cats and dogs in the field, but we are good at getting to the heart of a story.

In the correspondent-producer relationship, trust is the most important asset. There will be screw-ups covering assignments—especially when you haven't slept or eaten and feel the pressure to perform—but we can make decisions faster and more confidently because of the trust that we have built. Peter and I can spend an hour arguing over how to approach a story, but at the end of the day, we don't have the luxury of dwelling because we have to make TV.

From celebrating my birthday on the road to knowing when I need my personal space to have a good cry since my dad's passing, he's helped me get back on my feet at work.

"Please start eating your breakfast," he said to me as we all stumbled into the kitchen in our hurricane gear with barely enough time to make some coffee. After more than a year working together, he knows if I don't eat breakfast I will be very cranky. One needs energy for live television, especially to walk and talk in eighty-mile-per-hour winds. But in my case, I can't just have any random cereal or bagel; breakfast is one my rituals.

Rituals—there aren't many of those in the life of a breaking-news correspondent. You are home one minute, and the next you could be heading into a mass shooting, natural disaster, or political protest and not know when you'll be back home.

We all have our sad lists of canceled birthdays, nonappearances at parties, and unused concert tickets.

I live out of a carry-on. I have spent one out of every four nights in the past year at Marriott Hotels (and we don't always stay at a Marriott). I have status on almost all airlines. In short, I have no scheduled routine. Except for breakfast.

So here is my ritual:

Two slices of whole wheat bread, peanut butter, and sliced-up banana with lots of honey. I take my coffee black with only three drops of milk. (Where I come from we like our *cafecitos* strong.)

Whenever I order my coffee like this, Peter has a look on his face as though he just died a little inside.

To my surprise, I've recently found out I'm not that original. My breakfast is essentially the same as what Elvis Presley had for breakfast, with added bacon and apparently mayonnaise: "The Elvis Presley Sandwich." Fit for a king. Or the "Mariana Power Breakfast" version.

If I know I'm headed into a hurricane, I usually carry my breakfast with me. Everyone has their own little mechanisms to cope with the chaos around them. Tricks to stay sane on the road. Life can be so unpredictable in journalism that even one tiny stable detail can be a life preserver in a flood.

But for me, any sacrifice is worth it. After all, you see people going through some of the worst circumstances but also showing enormous displays of solidarity and resilience. You can't help but feel inspired.

I dealt with the emotional loss of losing my dad by throwing myself into this work. Connecting with people helped me find my father, even amid tragedy.

In the past years, I've covered six big storms, a couple of tornados, and one major earthquake. I've traveled to more than three dozen states and cities and told the stories of almost four thousand people who died, and thousands more left living in the aftermath.

When I started working as a reporter, I thought that being first and finding the truth were my main goals. I was wrong. That is just my job. What matters most to me now is to make people care, not just to hear the news and go on with their lives, thinking, *That's so sad. Fortunately it didn't happen to me.* I would like to make

everyone understand that eventually something like that can happen to any of us.

The world is shrinking. Our lives are more and more intercon-
nected by nature, technology, and politics. The good and the bad that
happens everywhere will affect us at some point. I see it every day.

The folks in the Carolinas were expecting life-threatening flooding, which some predicted could be as devastating as Hurricane
Harvey's destruction in Texas just a year before, in 2017.

Harvey was a historic storm, leaving 200,000 flooded homes
in Houston alone. The shelters for those who lost everything were
bursting at the seams. The faces of the rescued showed a mix of
gratitude and sorrow. It was heartbreaking.

News crews were mainly stationed in Houston. The world *was*
watching, but they were missing a lot. During our Harvey coverage,
Peter and I decided to drive south, where smaller cities were going
through similar conditions and fewer networks were reporting. We
spent days crisscrossing southeast Texas all the way to Louisiana,
stopping in Bridge City, Vidor City, and Beaumont.

We finally got to a tiny town called Rose. We were the only
national camera crew there. After hours of walking and shooting
interviews in the blazing sun, I went into the only place that was
open: a little hardware store.

"Psst! They found something in the water nearby," the owner
told me surreptitiously.

"What do you mean something?" I asked.

"A body," he said.

"What? Today?" This was two weeks after the storm. Officially, everyone had been accounted for.

"Is there any way we can find the place? We have to tell this story."

He drew a map for us.

We hopped in the car and rushed through the dirt roads, guided only by the piece of paper, until finally we spotted the police cars.

They had just taken the body out of the water. We decided not to report on this; we knew people in the area were still looking for lost loved ones, and the cops couldn't give us more precise information.

People were still dying, while others were still trying to find loved ones or venturing out to get drinking water for their children because the water pumps were flooded and the supply was gone. But their stories weren't being told. These people were too far, too few, and too poor to attract coverage.

I kept thinking, *Is anyone searching for this man? Does anyone care? Do I report this, even though my information is incomplete?*

I felt powerless.

There is no blueprint for what to do in those circumstances. You're dealing with people's lives. And they stay with you, always, no matter who they are.

When we covered Hurricane Irma in Florida in August of 2017, we were live in the middle of the *TODAY Show* on NBC when I spotted a homeless man from where we were filming. No jacket. No shoes. He reminded me of a leaf drifting in the wind.

I pointed him out while I was on the air. Millions of people watched as he held on to the wall of a boarded-up TGI Fridays, holding on for his life.

Our crew was about 150 feet away on a parking structure, actively trying to get down to him. But with the wind, it seemed like 150 miles.

I picked up my phone, called the authorities, and gave them the address where he was standing: "Ocean Drive and 5th Street. We will try to get to him, but please come now."

Suddenly when I looked down, he had disappeared. There was no trace of him, as though he had been sucked up by the hurricane.

I felt I had failed. Again. I told the world about him. But had I really done anything to help him?

These people left a profound impression on me, despite not knowing them. I later saw our recordings from those days and felt sick at how detached I looked. That's not at all how I felt, but I wasn't showing empathy, and some comments on social media even said I probably didn't care because he was homeless.

As human beings, we often find ourselves confronted with labels—*poor, homeless, mentally ill.* In my case, *immigrant, Latina, short* . . . We all have labels in our own minds or from the way others see us. We have to constantly remind ourselves to see a person, not a label.

As storytellers, we have to show what we feel. We have to make the pain real to the viewers. If we remain emotionless, so will the audience. Long gone is the era of the cold reporter who couldn't express feelings. Objectivity and compassion can go hand in hand.

Back in Oak Island, North Carolina, I was in the middle of Hurricane Florence. I couldn't make out what Peter was yelling from a distance, but I knew from his body language that he was reeling me in.

"Mariana, get back in the car, now!"

The water was a couple of feet deep. There was debris flying around. The sand was pounding my face and body to the point where it was hard to move.

I didn't feel any of it. I was feeding on pure adrenaline.

All the guys were in the SUV. My cameraman was shooting from the back of the car. I was the only woman and the only one out there bracing this thing: wobbling, talking—or trying to talk—about things like storm surge and the force of the winds, while showing our audience the damage in real time. It was an empowering feeling.

"Who do you think you are? Wonder Woman?" Peter shook his head as I jumped back in the SUV soaked as a wet chicken.

I wanted to keep filming but understood he was trying to protect us. We'd been going live all day on nothing but tuna and Gatorade in eighty-mile-per-hour winds, and it was time to take shelter at Paul's.

Thankfully the area wasn't hit that hard. After the storm passed, we started saying our goodbyes.

It sounds crazy, but it was tough to leave Paul and his house on the island. In a short time, he became part of our *familia* on the road.

I thought about my own family and how we were trying to find shelter from the storm after our devastating loss. Often we've found compassion in the eyes of onlookers; refuge in strangers who've lent a helping hand, or even, like Paul, some warm soup. I was paying attention to the signs. I saw Papi in Paul's smile too.

"Thank you for the past couple of days," Paul said to me as he gave me a hug and a warm cookie for the road. "It's been great to see this country from your eyes and your perspective."

Paul is a Trump supporter. The irony of helping and hosting the media in his house for days wasn't lost on us. He showed me that no matter how polarized the United States gets, love and kindness will prevail.

Three days after leaving the safety of Paul's home—and his nice washer and dryer—I had no more clean clothes.

Believe it or not, one of my biggest challenges about being on-air talent is what to wear. Concentrating on routines and the little things helps me better deal with the big stuff that comes my way. For instance, on TV I like to look different every day—an even bigger challenge for a correspondent who covers everything, because I am not always in the comfort of a studio. I can be launched into anything spur of the moment, in all types of weather. So I need clothes for storms, fires, protests, politics, sit-down interviews, you name it.

And I have to fit everything in a carry-on. Checking bags only complicates last-minute flight changes.

Some reporters get year-round stylists, but those are expensive.

What do I do? I have my closet organized in distinctive stacks, labeled with stickers that read: "Interviews," "Protests & Riots," "Airport/Travel," and the like. It allows me to grab stuff quickly depending on the assignment and not think twice about it.

I don't buy expensive clothes. I don't care about labels. With time, I've learned a practical wardrobe is about being comfortable enough to let your personality show—and about the fit. At five foot three and a hundred pounds, I can either look as if I've been swallowed by an oversized sack of potatoes or, with the right fit and colors, feel like my favorite female superhero.

But honestly, these are only little tools to toughen up. Life on the road is an emotional roller coaster. In a matter of seconds you can go from cheering your team on because you were able to be live on TV from a place nobody had covered to consoling an interviewee in the worst moment of his or her life.

Mexico, September 2017

My most heart-wrenching coverages have also been the ones where I feel I've been able to contribute the most, which is hard to reconcile. The biggest struggle is accepting praise when lives have been lost—like the summer when a 7.1-magnitude earthquake shattered Mexico City in 2017. All it took was twenty seconds for homes, employment centers, and entire blocks to come crumbling down.

I knew it would be hard to get there. This wasn't a domestic story for the American public. Since many of the victims and witnesses didn't speak English, it would be more challenging to convey their suffering. I pushed hard, and finally the network agreed to send me down there.

Hundreds were dead. Nineteen children had been crushed in a primary school. Volunteers searched through the destruction, and dogs were sniffing for life. Every second counted because dozens were trapped underneath the rubble. There was still hope.

Rescue workers needed all the help they could get. They needed teams, experts, and supplies to be sent from abroad. The United States and countries as far away as Spain, Japan, and Israel stepped in to help.

I put on my hard hat. I could barely breathe. There were aftershocks, and we feared that the structures around us would start shaking again.

In the beginning, Peter told me, "I don't know how you are going to do this in Spanish and English." I wasn't sure either, but I let my instincts take control. I started translating on air in a very casual and organic manner. People would tell me their names and stories and what they needed in Spanish, and I would repeat it in English. We went into almost every rescue site and spent entire days broadcasting the dread, but also the hope, in two languages.

Fortunately, we saw progress when help from international aid organizations like the American Red Cross and private donations kept pouring in.

On day four, I talked to a father who had lost his child at the Enrique Rébsamen primary school. The boy's nickname was Paquito, and he was just seven years old. I will never forget what this man told me. "Paquito was a great kid, *un tipazo*, and now he's gone." Tears spilled from his eyes as the camera kept rolling. At that moment Paquito's father, in a church in Mexico City, made people thousands of miles away connect to a pain that wasn't theirs. Even if we haven't experienced a massive earthquake, we all know what loss feels like.

Paquito's father thanked me, and I could sincerely accept his gratitude and give him mine for his bravery in opening his heart to a stranger.

Back at 30 Rockefeller, the response from my bosses and colleagues was encouraging. I thought about how I pushed to get the story on the air. I had finally found my place in that iconic building in New York, which had been so intimidating when I first started, by being myself and telling the story the way it deserved to be told: humbly, with raw emotion that really needed no translation.

Puerto Rico, September 2017

That summer I hardly recovered from the emotional toll of covering the earthquake in Mexico when our team got sent to Puerto Rico. I had visited the beautiful island before, but now it looked completely different: devastated after Hurricane Maria.

I spent weeks talking to *boricuas*, or Puerto Ricans, who had not only lost homes but their entire way of life.

Their main complaint was that even though they were American citizens, they were not being treated as such. The government was not responding to the disaster the way it had responded to equivalent disasters on the mainland US. Actually, polls have shown that almost half of Americans don't even know Puerto Ricans are US citizens. News of President Trump throwing paper towels, imitating a Puerto Rican accent, or fighting with San Juan mayor Carmen Yulín Cruz was everywhere; but there, on the ground, I could see the only thing that really mattered: Puerto Ricans were not getting the help they needed.

I didn't know what else I could do. I knew the story was reaching its expiration date. Competition is fierce, and networks move on to the next thing quickly. Nowadays it's hard for a story to stay in the headlines for more than a week. Even though this one was so close to home, there was no cultural affinity. Puerto Rico's main language is Spanish, and aside from all the political commotion, the English media was losing interest.

One day I walked through a line of about a thousand people desperate for ice, medicine, and food. Some started gathering around me, and when they realized I was reporting, they yelled, "¡*Puerto Rico se levanta!* Puerto Rico rises!"

People smiled and clapped and gave each other hugs. They gave *me* the strength to keep going and to bring their spirit to television and Instagram, Twitter, Facebook, and Snapchat.

Often I think of all those stories I haven't covered: the brutal displacement of the Rohingya Muslims in Myanmar, the terrorist attacks in Europe, the crisis in Nicaragua. I wish I could do more.

But I've also learned that quality over quantity is not a cliché; it's the most respectful way to show we care. I had the opportunity to spend time and form bonds with the protagonists of my stories. They left an imprint that will never fade. Telling their stories was a privilege I was ready to fight for.

If there's anything I learned during this time, it's to focus on what you are willing to fight for; then go ahead and do it, whatever it takes—no matter the risk. We only need to care enough to come forward, like the women who have said #MeToo, the DREAMers who refuse to yield, the Puerto Ricans fighting to preserve their island and way of life, and my Venezuelan *paisanos* who fight every day without surrendering. Even Paul Gawin, our host during Hurricane Florence, a stranger who, with a simple act of kindness, reminded me that no matter what labels we put on each other, we can find shelter—and human connection—in the storm.

#*Go like Mariana*: We all have labels in our own minds or from the way others see us. We have to constantly remind ourselves to see a person, not a label.

#*Go like Mariana*: Focus on what you are willing to fight for; then do it.

14

Breaking the Mold

In 2018, I got engrossed in royal wedding fever, like almost every other person on the planet. The UK's Prince Harry is exactly my age. I vividly recall his somber face on the day of Princess Diana's funeral and the handwritten note atop the casket that read "Mum."

As he grew older, we all fell in love with his cheeky smile, his warmth and kindness, and wondered who would snag the world's most eligible bachelor. He was mostly seen with beautiful—usually blonde—society girls. But Harry didn't end up with the sort of bride everyone thought he would choose.

Prince Harry married Meghan Markle, an American actress, who is a divorcée, was raised by a single mom, and, most importantly, is a woman of color—the first one in modern history to enter the revered circle of the British royal family.

Harry didn't fall in love with Meghan because she was perfect but because she was real. And her empathy means so much to a lot of people—not just in the UK but around the world. From kneeling down to hug children in the streets at eye level, to being an impassioned public speaker who doesn't like to use the barrier of a lectern, to cooking for the homeless at the Hubb Community Kitchen in West London, Meghan locks eyes with everyday people and connects in a meaningful way, long after the traditional photo op.

Meghan has the power to be a role model who can walk in someone else's shoes—to navigate both worlds. A modern-day superhero. No title can buy that.

Watching them, I can't help but think about my own royal encounters—with the king and queen of Spain and with the pope himself. In these situations, protocol and tradition were *de rigueur*. But it's those everyday, human connections—being real—that break down the walls that divide "us" and "them." We're all perfectly human, after all.

Miami, 2013

Felipe and Letizia of Spain, an elegant and dashing-looking couple, were touring the United States on an official visit and stopped by

Univision Network's new facilities in Miami, at the time deemed "the most modern newsroom in America."

Letizia—like Meghan—was a "commoner" before she married the future king and was also a divorcée and a well-known journalist in her day. Maybe the interest for their newsroom visit sparked there.

Upon their entrance, the open-planned, perennially busy, and loud newsroom was at a standstill. You only heard whispers and the sounds of royal photographers clicking away with their cameras. Followed by their entourage, a robust security detail, and throng of onlookers, the future king and queen strolled around with grace, as if they walked on a cloud.

Impulsive as I am, I went ahead and introduced myself.

"*Hola*, I am Mariana," I said to his highness casually. "I am a journalist like you," I told his wife with pride. (I thought it would be nice to recognize her as a professional woman, not just someone with an acquired title.)

The entourage and crowds who were walking around them in a sort of spread-out circle let out hushed "oohs" and an orchestra of "OMGs!"

Whoops. What did I do?

I turned around and noticed many of the people around us were bowing or bending their necks. Some of the women were even doing a small curtsy.

"Errr, Your Majesty," I added to soften the blow.

I wondered why I had never read a manual on how to greet a member of a royal family (and those *do* exist in fair abundance).

"When did you know you wanted to be a journalist?" the future queen asked. "What motivated you?" his highness followed.

What? They actually wanted to talk to me?

In retrospect, I think talking to them like they were real people actually broke through.

Well, two could play at the question game. "When did *you* know you wanted to be a king? What motivated *you*?" I replied with a sly smile. He widened his eyes, surprised.

His Majesty laughed. It was a real laugh too. Then I took one more chance to do something unexpected.

"Can I take a selfie with you, sir?" I asked. "My *abuelita* would be very proud."

When I took my cell phone out for the first royal selfie the king of Spain ever took, the tough guys from his security detail got ready to pounce on me. But His Majesty stopped them cold with one small gesture.

"¡*Vamos!*" he said to me as he smiled for the photo.

The moment went viral. As common as they are now, selfies were a new thing back then. (In fact, *selfie* beat *twerk* as the word of the year in 2013.) The most important newspaper in Spain, *El País*, featured the photo, as did a ton of other publications, as a "refreshing new look for a traditional and stuffy institution."

The headlines read: "A Renovated Monarchy, for a New Time," and, "The Journalist Who Dared Ask the King for a Selfie."

I sent the photo to Papi so he would show my grandma. He was so proud.

"You broke royal protocol!" he texted me. "And I broke the mold when I made you," he added, with a little crown emoji.

When I first told him I wanted to be a journalist, he gave

me this advice: "Become an example and an ambassador for this generation of change you will always belong to."

The day of my royal encounter I broke through, not by being perfect, but by being perfectly me, and seeing people as human beings, beyond labels.

As I write these last pages, a migrant caravan of thousands of desperate families has been held on the Mexican side of the US border, seeking asylum, while President Donald Trump is threatening to militarize the area. We have reported on young children with disabilities who are being made to wait in a place where they feel unsafe because, "Sorry, America is full."

I'm pushing to go back down there and report live on TV to show that these migrants are not "the other." They are human beings. I will continue to humanize the immigration debate to make audiences see these people as more than "illegal" aliens.

US–Mexico Border, 2015

This issue also came up in the summer of 2015, during another royal encounter of sorts—this one of the spiritual kind—with Pope Francis.

ABC News had secured a virtual audience with the pope from three cities across the United States, before his first official visit to America. The focus was to uplift marginalized communities, a signature cause of Pope Francis.

David Muir would anchor from the Vatican, while Tom Llamas would be in Chicago with young students and Cecilia Vega in Los Angeles with people who were homeless. ABC needed someone who understood migrant families and spoke Spanish and English. Even though I was younger than the rest of the anchors and correspondents, and didn't officially work for ABC News, they picked me.

I was to host the dozens of migrants at a church showing the pope live on a big-screen TV. I would introduce his holiness to the families and facilitate questions in Spanish all while taping a broadcast in English for the ABC show *20/20*.

Every time you ask migrants what gets them through the journey, after having walked more than two thousand miles to get to the border, many of whom have been extorted, raped, and beaten, they'll answer with one word: *fe*. Faith.

What I remember most about the papal audience was seeing their faces when I got to tell them that after all they endured, they would get to see and talk to the pope. Their smiles could have lit up a room. It was a reaffirmation of faith. Their journey and suffering suddenly felt justified.

"*¡Ayyyy Bendito!* God is smiling down on us!" one mom cried as she hugged me.

On the day of the broadcast, the little church in McAllen, Texas, was packed—with people and with faith. I felt it.

"Ladies and gentlemen, let's give a warm welcome to Pope Francis!" I said.

Clapping, cheering, and tears erupted, sounds reverberating through the stalls.

"Your Holiness, my name is Mariana Atencio. I am a journalist." As I introduced myself I also felt, like the migrants, that my own journey was justified.

I introduced the pope to a ten-year-old girl named Wendy, who burst into tears in the middle of the broadcast while telling him what she had endured coming to the US. This little girl had confessed to me earlier that she had watched her mom being raped by gangs along the way.

It broke my heart. I told her that they were both incredibly brave and would find a way to heal.

When she started talking to the pope, she was crying so much she couldn't speak. I told her to breathe. From the corner of my eye, I saw that Wendy's mom was holding one of her stick-figure drawings.

"Why don't you show his holiness what you made for him?" I asked her.

The little girl grabbed the cardboard live on TV and proudly displayed it for Pope Francis. He smiled, with a genuine belly laugh that lit up the whole church again.

"¡*Gracias!*" the pope said.

Thousands of parents watching all over the country saw their own children reflected in that stick-figure drawing. The papal audience aired as an hour-long *20/20* special that later won a Gabriel Award from the Catholic Press Association.

Once again, authenticity broke down another wall that divides "us" and "them." That's a way of changing the world, one heart at a time.

I think I've always been a wall breaker. (And remember: where there's breaking involved, it hurts and you bleed.) As a teenager I imagined myself like Princess Leia trying to save the world from the dark side. By the time Katniss Everdeen entered our culture, those dreams had evolved into something more realistic. My path as a journalist was very clear, but still sprinkled with the same desire to do something to make the world a better place.

Little by little I learned that using my voice motivates others to use theirs, leading to positive change—and that is a superpower all of us have.

Covering the crisis at the border, I learned that individually and collectively we need to improve our relationships. It takes courage to show respect. Like Voltaire, I believe that even though I might not agree with what you have to say, I'll defend to the death your right to say it. We cannot love everybody, but we should respect everybody.

Failing to see anything good in a person who thinks differently makes a dialogue impossible. Without dialogue we will keep repeating the same mistakes because we will not learn anything new.

How do we put ourselves in Wendy's shoes? How do we make sure she knows she's special and not simply "unworthy" of having a family or a chance at life? By showing her and people like her on a national network, and by speaking with them in their own language, I tried to make viewers see them not as "illegal" aliens but as human beings. Yes, they broke the law by committing a misdemeanor and will have to pay a penalty for that, but they have also sacrificed everything to have a chance at a better life in this country, as many other immigrants throughout history have.

Let's stop finding flaws and start looking for meaningful connections.

Review your story and think of those moments when you or anyone you love was "the other."

We all come to this world in a body. People with physical or neurological difficulties, those who are part of environmentally affected communities, immigrants, boys who want to dress as girls, girls with veils, women who have been sexually assaulted, athletes who bend their knees as a sign of protest, blacks, whites, Native Americans—you and me.

We all want what everyone wants: the chance to live our best lives, to dream, and to achieve.

But sometimes society tells us, and we tell ourselves, that we are unworthy because we don't fit an ideal. If you look at my story— from being born somewhere "different," to dancing for charity in high school, getting tear-gassed for democracy, and telling stories you wouldn't normally see on TV—what makes me different is what has made me successful. And ultimately, fulfilled.

I have traveled all over the world and met people from all walks of life, and I've come to one conclusion: being human is the only thing every single one of us has in common. The way we deal with our differences—other people's and our own—will define how we live.

#Go like Mariana: Little by little I learned that using my voice motivates others to use theirs, leading to positive change—and that is a superpower all of us have.

Epilogue

An Open-Ended Story

Every person has a story worth sharing. In fact, we are all story-tellers. When we say "I had a vivid dream last night" or "Something wonderful happened to me this morning," we are actively weaving the narrative of humankind. So, after being asked many times about my journey, from fleeing a dictatorship in South America and moving to the United States in search of a new life, to fulfilling my American dream of becoming a journalist, I finally decided to share my story in print.

It wasn't easy. My closest relatives are very private and had a hard time with the idea of me writing about our lives. Publishing it would make our story open to anyone, even to those we call "haters" on social media. I'm sure they'll have plenty to pick at from these pages. And I'm fine with that, because every time I tell people bits and pieces of my story, they always seem to find something that takes them back to their own personal or family histories. Those interactions are the best examples of how positive, empowering, and liberating it is to connect our experiences as humans.

In these pages I've shared the magical place of my childhood, ripped from me as I struggled against tear gas and tyranny. I've told you what it was like to feel different at summer camp thousands of miles away from home, then win a scholarship to an Ivy League school, only to get fired from my first job. And then later, how I got the gig of my dreams and a devastating car crash almost tore my family into pieces but brought us together at the same time. I wanted to share the stories of so many people I've found and lost along the way, especially Papi, who will always be my guiding light. He taught me that being real was my superpower, and I have learned to use it.

I still fight not to be stereotyped. Labeled. Put in a box. But today I know I am meant to expand, to become a human bridge and to try to make a difference through my storytelling, sharing all the detours and roadblocks I faced in times of uncertainty to help others see that they, too, can overcome any obstacle to reach their goals.

All the stories I've covered in my career made me understand that if we as peoples, cultures, and humans don't find a way to embrace our differences and rid ourselves of the fear of the other, we will never be able to benefit from peace, freedom, and happiness.

Perhaps I can say this because I have been shown human tragedy and true resilience from life teachers, especially all those strong women who have shaped my identity. From my mom, Diana Atencio, the Queen of Naiguatá and Fatima, to little Wendy and Angelina, to María Elena Salinas and Graciela.

After her accident I pushed to cover Ferguson in the summer of 2014. There, my eyes were opened to the pain and suffering of the African American community in the United States. I hadn't seen such disparity since I left my home country. But the tear gas, the police repression, and the divisions were achingly familiar.

I encountered those things again when I reported on protests in Hong Kong (summer 2014), Mexico's murdered students in Ayotzinapa (fall 2014), and Haiti's earthquake and cholera survivors (January 2015). Watching Gracie's recovery had given me a special sensibility, and I thought about her whenever I approached people who were suffering. I am constantly astounded by the human ability to adapt and overcome, especially in this country.

I am not a US citizen on paper yet. But I've spent the majority of my career covering the frontlines of the changing face of America. At every turn, I meet people who put kindness first, who welcome dialogue.

Like Paul Gawin in North Carolina, who took us in and sheltered us from a hurricane instead of calling us "fake news" and telling us to get lost.

And like Pastor Ray Sanders, a conservative voter and educator I interviewed at the 2018 Oklahoma teachers' strike. After we finished filming, he learned it was my birthday and that I had just lost my father. The next day, Ray came back, braving the crowds for hours to get up to the third floor of the Capitol building, where our cameras were positioned, to give me something I will treasure forever.

Along with a bouquet of flowers and a balloon, he handed me a framed message that surely came from the heavens: "To my daughter . . . No matter where life takes you . . . I'll always stand beside you, loving you, supporting you, and encouraging you."

On the back of the frame, Ray added a personal note with a black magic marker:

"As a father, I think this is what your daddy wants you to always know."

Pastor Ray Sanders will have a special place in my heart forever.

I continue to share stories online and on social media about the Pauls and Rays of the world, about assimilating in America, and even about losing Papi. The response has been overwhelming. The tsunami of messages from all over the world and the positive response to my TEDx Talks show that people of all ages and backgrounds are celebrating what makes them different and sharing it with others, creating a perfectly you way to make us more powerful—as individuals and communities.

We cannot let our faults, perceived disadvantages, differences, or weaknesses keep us silent or separated. Everyone feels different sometimes, but we can find unity and give back. Being perfectly you is the foundation for giving our best to the world. It is a gift of love.

I choose to believe that we all want the same things. It's what attracted me to come to this country in the first place. It's what I know as fundamental to the human spirit.

So what's left for me to do? You have every right to ask.

Well, I'm currently sitting in my mom's new apartment in Caracas, adjusting to its air. The streets of the city today feel almost unrecognizable. A lot of my friends have fled. Mami sold our childhood home to get some closure. I'm here on an emergency trip after my only official document, my Venezuelan passport, was stolen during our midterm election coverage in Houston in the fall of 2018. I had to get a special permit to travel here and get a new one issued. In Venezuela, battling the bureaucracy is an Orwellian task.

I'm stranded. But now I know that nothing ever happens by mistake. There's always a higher purpose.

Since I can't sit idle, I've filled my days bringing food and medicine to children in the poor barrios. With every spoonful of liquid vitamin they take, I've asked them to tell me what they want to be when they grow up. "Veterinarian!" "Firefighter!" "Actress!" they yelled.

In their answers I saw that sharing their dreams out loud energizes them. It's storytelling at its most sincere. Long before we put our stories in writing, we talk about them, we play around with ways to tell them, or we fantasize about the future, which in turn will enable us to achieve our dreams.

In Caracas, I also gave a lecture on being "Perfectly You" to the hundreds of scholarship recipients from our DAR Learning platform, the social media e-course site that launched in 2018. The auditorium was filled with more than four hundred local men and women looking for inspiration amid the crisis. I saw in them the same desire as the kids: to rise above the circumstances and find their purpose.

In my time here, it dawned on me that with so many things coming full circle, I had to go back to the beginning. I had to go back to El Ávila Mountain.

It had been eleven years since the mugging, and I hadn't set foot there since. Even now, if I close my eyes, I can still see the man who put a gun to my head standing over me. Sure, I had lived through so many other things, possibly far more dangerous. I had experienced bigger fears—and yet this one was in a category all its own. But I knew I owed myself the chance to finally overcome my trauma and put it behind me.

I went through a routine somewhat similar to the one I'd followed that day, looking for my sneakers and running around the house. This time Mami was out, so she wouldn't be able to object. I left the apartment, and a friend drove me to the trail's entrance in a bulletproof car. It seemed ridiculous, since it's five minutes away, but this is the new normal here. I got out nervously. No car or guard or armored anything was standing in my way. I looked at everyone around me, trying to figure out if they were dangerous. *Dale, Mariana—it's going to be okay.*

Count to one hundred, I said to myself as I recalled that moment on the mountain trail when the gun pressing against my skin forced me to make a decision that would change my life.

Uno . . . I started to climb. The first couple of steps were awkward. As I felt my pace quicken and my heart beat faster, I remembered exactly where I was going. With every turn I connected with nature, noticing the sound of the birds. *There you are, Papi*, I thought as I kept climbing the steep hill.

People were everywhere. It was still the refuge it had always been to Venezuelans of all walks of life. Seeing men stare at me made me nervous. I've heard stories of others getting robbed even amid the crowds. *Cincuenta y uno, cincuenta y dos, cincuenta y tres . . .* I continued my way up, feeling an evolution occurring within me with every step I took.

The strength I had accumulated since that terrifying moment had kept growing. The world had opened up for me in the best of ways. Before I knew it . . . *Noventa y ocho, noventa y nueve, cien*—one hundred! There I was, standing at the place where a total stranger took control of my life. And I was no longer afraid.

Continuing to the viewpoint, I looked beyond the horizon at the city below me. I could feel a sense of wonder and wholeness. I finally understood why I needed to come back here. As the poet Rumi said, the wound is the place where the light enters you.

The light led me to find my purpose.

We all have a strong suit, something we are good at, for the service of others, which can only be achieved through power, love, and a sound mind, as the apostle Paul said. Mine was storytelling—being a human bridge in everything I do. Yours may come from the places you've been, the brokenness you've experienced, the divisions you've faced and overcome. I believe with all my heart that what makes you different is what makes you perfectly suited to give to the world.

As I headed down the mountain I was grateful that no matter where I went next, I was already equipped with a toolkit of hard-earned lessons. As long as I didn't forget who I was, I'd thrive on the ride. Wherever or whatever was next, I just couldn't forget the most valuable lesson of all: show up as myself. Because everyone else is already taken.

Watch out, world. I'm ready to #GoLikeMariana!

And I invite you to do the same, with your own name—your own story.

#GoLike _____.

Acknowledgments

Mirna, your name means "peace," but you are a warrior of light against fear and self-doubt. Thanks for being the shield that protects me from negativity. This book is yours as much as mine.

Jose, *mi amor*, my soul mate. Without you I feel lost. Thanks for your love, patience, the insightful details that help me see the other side of the story, and the warm hugs that only you can give me. *¡Te amo!*

Mami, having you as a role model is the best gift a daughter could ask for. I'm forever grateful to have your support, strength, and unconditional love. You are my rock! Thanks for encouraging me to be *perfectly me*.

Graciela, you grew from little sister and my better half to the most admirable woman and the strongest person I know. Learning from you is a wonderful privilege, and I appreciate every minute I get to spend with you. Do we still get to trade everything in our closets?

Alvaro Elias, thanks for standing by me through thick and thin. You took care of us just as Papi would have wanted you to do. I know how proud he is of the man you have become. I don't say it often enough, but I adore you little brother. You are really special.

Ali and Cait, words can't express my gratitude for everything you guys did to make this book a reality. Thanks so much for being friends before agents, for trusting me, guiding me every step of the way, and making me feel comfortable when we had to juggle hard decisions.

Verónica and Maickel, my BFFs and social media gurus, thanks for sharing your wealth of knowledge with me since I started navigating the digital world, and for instilling in me the importance of posting responsibly with respect and humanity. Those lessons are also a big part of this book. Insert praying hands emoji here!

Jenn and Meaghan, I am immensely grateful for all the sound notes, the spectacular editing, and masterfully moving around the pieces of this puzzle until everything made sense. I am still in awe of how well you translated my emotions into these pages.

Matt, your generosity and enthusiasm mean the world to me. The first time we spoke I knew we had found a champion for our message and a true Renaissance man who also appreciates 61.4 percent dark chocolate. Thank you for your faithful support.

Megan, your wonderful supervision kept us on track when

hurricanes, midterm elections, and other news coverages threatened to derail us. Gracias for holding our hands to steadily take us to a safe port.

Daisy, Denise, Cris, and everyone at W Publishing, thanks for putting up with our crazy schedules and for understanding our need to rewrite, adapt, and make last-minute changes in both English and Spanish. I'm grateful for your contributions and warm messages. They made all the difference.

Kristen, your artistic eye, excellent taste, and critical thinking gave this book a first-rate cover. Thanks for this lovely design that fits my colorful, quirky personality. Not an easy feat!

And most importantly, thank you, *mi gente*—dear Reader—for taking this book home in any form you choose. You rock!

Notes

Chapter 3: "Please Don't Look Too Latina"

34 Latinos are the largest minority in the US: Statistics on the growth of the US Hispanic population can be found at "Percentage Distribution of Population in the United States in 2015 and 2060, by Race and Hispanic Origin," Statista.org, accessed January 25, 2019, https://www.statista.com/statistics/270272/percentage -of-us-population-by-ethnicities/; and Jens Manuel Krogstad, "With Fewer New Arrivals, Census Lowers Hispanic Population Projections," Pew Research Center, December 16, 2014, http:// www.pewresearch.org/fact-tank/2014/12/16/with-fewer-new -arrivals-census-lowers-hispanic-population-projections-2/.

36 "prejudicial or preferential treatment": Alice Walker's definition of *colorism* can be found in her book *In Search of Our Mothers'*

Gardens: Womanist Prose (New York: Harcourt Brace Jovanovich, 1983), 290. For more on colorism, see Kimberly Jade Norwood, "'If You Is White, You's Alright. . . .' Stories About Colorism in America," vol. 14 Washington University Global Studies Law Review 585 (2015), http://openscholarship.wustl.edu/law_globalstudies/vol14/iss4/8.

37 **fifty-eight million Hispanics in the US:** Statistics on the current number of Hispanics in the US can be found at the Pew Research Center's website, in Antonio Flores, "How the US Hispanic Population Is Changing," Pew Research Center Fact Tank, September 18, 2017, http://www.pewresearch.org/fact-tank/2017/09/18/how-the-u-s-hispanic-population-is-changing/.

Chapter 4: A Human Bridge

58 **"Iraq, North Korea, Iran":** George W. Bush's words on the "axis of evil" can be found in his State of the Union Address, delivered at the US Capitol, Washington, DC, January 29, 2002. The transcript is posted online at https://georgewbush-whitehouse.archives.gov/news/releases/2002/01/20020129-11.html.

58 **"We are more alike":** Maya Angelou's famous line "We are more alike, my friends, than we are unalike," is from her poem "Human Family," in *I Shall Not Be Moved: Poems* (New York: Random House, 1990), 4.

Chapter 6: Mariana the Journalist

80 **114,000 newsroom employees:** Pew Research Center statistics on job loss among newsroom employees can be found in Elizabeth Grieco, "Newsroom Employment Dropped Nearly a Quarter in Less Than 10 Years, with Greatest Decline at Newspapers," Pew Research Center Fact Tank, July 30, 2018, http://www.pewresearch.org/fact-tank/2018/07/30/newsroom-employment-dropped-nearly-a-quarter-in-less-than-10-years-with-greatest-decline-at-newspapers/.

87 journalism is telling people about other people: Masha Gessen's thoughts on journalism can be found in her article "How to Tell the Stories of Immigration," *Atlantic*, December 5, 2018, https://www.theatlantic.com/ideas/archive/2018/12/masha-gessen-wins-2018-hitchens-prize/577297/.

Chapter 7: The Yes Attitude

106 "under the nose of a regime": Yoani Sánchez's quotation about freedom of speech can be found in Oscar Hijuelos, "Heroes and Pioneers: Yoani Sánchez," *Time*, May 12, 2018, http://content.time.com/time/specials/2007/artic le/0,28804,1733748_1733756_1735878,00.html.

Chapter 10: A World of Separation

152 "When Mexico sends its people": Full text of Donald Trump's announcement of his presidential bid, including his comments on Mexicans, is posted online at "Full Text: Donald Trump Announces a Presidential Bid," *Washington Post*, June 16, 2015, https://www.washingtonpost.com/news/post-politics/wp/2015/06/16/full-text-donald-trump-announces-a-presidential-bid/?noredirect=on&utm_term=.63532a885534.

152 Donald Trump won the presidency: For more about the electoral college victory, see Andrew Rafferty, "Electoral College Vote Seals Trump White House Victory," NBC News, December 19, 2016, https://www.nbcnews.com/politics/politics-news/electoral-college-vote-seals-trump-white-house-victory-n698026.

152 ICE (Immigration and Customs Enforcement) raided many businesses: Reporting on ICE raids and activities in 2018 can be found in Corky Siemaszko, "Immigration Agents Raid 7-Eleven Stores Nationwide, Arrest 21 People in Biggest Crackdown of Trump Era," NBC News, January 10, 2018, https://www.nbcnews.com/news/us-news/immigration-agents-raid-7-eleven-stores-nationwide-arrest-21-people-n836531.

152 **"fairly adjudicating requests"**: The new mission statement of
the US Citizens and Immigration Services can be found at their
website, "About Us," accessed January 18, 2019, https://www.uscis
.gov/aboutus.

154 **Venezuela was now the most dangerous country in the world:**
Venezuela's status as the most dangerous country in the world
is covered in Emily Shugerman, "Venezuela Rated Least Safe
Country in the World for Second Year in a Row," *Independent*,
June 7, 2018, https://www.independent.co.uk/news/world
/americas/most-dangerous-country-venezuela-safe-south-america
-gallup-a8388736.html.

155 **"There is no agony like bearing an untold story inside you"**:
This line is from Zora Neale Hurston's memoir *Dust Tracks on a
Road: An Autobiography* (New York: HarperCollins, 1942; 1995),
176, though it is often attributed to Maya Angelou.

162 **ProPublica published the recorded audio:** ProPublica's audio
of six-year-old Alison Valencia Madrid was published by Ginger
Thompson, "Listen to Children Who've Just Been Separated
from Their Parents at the Border," June 18, 2018, ProPublica,
https://www.propublica.org/article/children-separated-from
-parents-border-patrol-cbp-trump-immigration-policy.

162 **"If you don't like that"**: Jeff Sessions's comments on family
separation at the border were reported by Pete Williams, "Sessions:
Parents, Children Entering US Illegally Will Be Separated," NBC
News, May 7, 2018, https://www.nbcnews.com/politics/justice
-department/sessions-parents-children-entering-us-illegally-will
-be-separated-n872081.

164 **I sat down with Cristina:** Our coverage from McAllen, Texas,
including interviews with Cristina, the mom from El Salvador,
aired on MSNBC's *Morning Joe*, June 19, 2018, and can be viewed
in part on YouTube at https://www.youtube.com/watch?v
=DjPEtfJNw2w.

166 **"We are fathers and brothers and human beings too"**: My

interview with border patrol agent Gabriel Acosta can be viewed online in Stephanie Ruhle, "How Border Patrol Agents Perform Their Work," MSNBC.com, https://www.msnbc.com /stephanie-ruhle/watch/how-border-patrol-agents-perform- their-work-1260998211939.

Chapter 11: A Million Likes for You

180 **"What Makes You Special?":** My TEDx Talk can be viewed at "What Makes You Special?", TEDx University of Nevada, April 2017, https://www.ted.com/talks/mariana_atencio_what_makes _you_special/up-next?language=en.

183 **March for Our Lives protest:** To view my reporting from this event, see "Students at the March for Our Lives Discuss Message in Front of White House," MSNBC, March 24, 2018, https://www.msnbc.com/msnbc/watch/students-at-the-march -for-our-lives-discuss-message-in-front-of-white-house -1194345539828.

Chapter 12: Losing My Dad and My Country

189 **a shortage of 85 percent of drugs in Venezuela:** Coverage of the drug shortage in Venezuela, including pharmaceutical association estimates, can be found in Anggy Polanco and Isaac Urrutia, "Venezuela's Chronic Shortages Give Rise to 'Medical Flea Markets,'" *Reuters*, December 8, 2017, https://www.reuters.com /article/us-venezuela-medicine/venezuelas-chronic-shortages-give -rise-to-medical-flea-markets-idUSKBN1E21J4.

196 **"Death is nothing at all":** The poem "Death Is Nothing At All" is by Henry Scott Holland in 1910, and is sometimes attributed to Saint Augustine.

198 **"In the Chaos of Venezuela":** My April 25, 2018, NBC News article "In the Chaos of Venezuela, a Daughter Fights for her Father's Life" can be found at https://www.nbcnews.com/specials /venezuelas-health-crisis.

Chapter 14: Breaking the Mold

219 **a "refreshing new look"**: You can see a Spanish-language report
about and pictures from our encounter at Almudena Martín,
"El príncipe Felipe se marca un 'selfie' con una periodista,"
El País, November 20, 2013, https://smoda.elpais.com
/imperdibles/2013/11/el-principe-felipe-se-marca-un-selfie/.

Epilogue

231 **the wound is the place where the light enters you:** Rumi's poem
"Childhood Friends" referring to light entering through wounds,
can be found in *The Essential Rumi*, Coleman Barks, trans.,
expanded edition (New York: HarperOne, 1995), 141.

About the Author

Mariana Atencio is a journalist, TED speaker, influencer, and award-winning news personality covering domestic and international assignments, breaking news, and special reports. As a first-generation Latina who fled violence and oppression in her native Venezuela, she crossed over from Spanish- to English-language television. Known for her tenacious reporting, she has been named one of the top young voices in American newsrooms, and her awards include the Peabody Award for Investigative Journalism, the Gracie Award, and the National Association of Hispanic Journalists "Latino Issues" Award. Her TEDx Talks have been seen by more than eight million people and translated in more than eight languages. She loves vintage movies, peanut butter, honey, and salsa dancing.